MEMORIES
OF THE
GREAT DEPRESSION

MADGE PETTIT

HERITAGE BOOKS
2006

HERITAGE BOOKS
AN IMPRINT OF HERITAGE BOOKS, INC.

Books, Cds, and more—Worldwide

For our listing of thousands of titles see our website
at
www.HeritageBooks.com

Published 2006 by
HERITAGE BOOKS, INC.
Publishing Division
65 East Main Street
Westminster, Maryland 21157-5026

International Standard Book Number: 978-0-7884-3363-6

...to the memory of my parents

Joe and Margie Seales

I

When the Axe Fell

The beginning of the Great Depression might be compared to a giant axe-blade descending upon the exposed neck of a victim. The victim in this case was the United States of America, and especially the already impoverished southeastern part of the nation. It happened in October of the year 1929. I had just turned nine years old at the time, the second oldest of the then five children. The youngest was only three months old, and two more were born during the dark years of economic depression that followed.

In 1929, our family was still firmly planted in the agricultural age, at a time in which most of the people in that area had long since moved into the industrial age. This proved to be a blessing in some respects as the Depression lengthened and deepened and dragged on and on for twelve years, or until the beginning of World War II. The economic history of the United States as the reader no doubt knows has happened in three distinct stages, or as we call them, ages. The first was the agricultural age, in which our society was founded. It was almost completely agrarian, and in the south, where schools were few, education was not given a high priority. What was important was the ownership of land and a willingness to work hard, and the latter applied to women as well as men. The women usually worked alongside the men clearing and tilling the land, building fences, tending the livestock and the other hard work of keeping a pioneer homestead running, besides taking care of the family and managing the household. It was also important that she be able to bear many children to help with the farm work.

The second age was the industrial age in which manufacturing and exports became all important. Large factories were built, largely in the north, but also sometimes in the south, and most people worked there, or more correctly, the men worked there. In our part of the country, steel mills and blast furnaces were the main sources of employment. The women stayed home, cooked, sewed, and raised the children. When a young man went looking for a wife, he looked for someone who was a good cook, and was possessed of a few

1

social graces. It was not considered essential for a female to be educated beyond secondary school, and the man more often than not "married down", choosing a wife who was younger, less well educated, and less affluent.

In the mid twentieth century, the Industrial age began giving way to the information age in which we now live. The great factories of the north were abandoned and became part of a "rust belt" which spread across the region and came to identify it, much as the more enticing "sun belt" had always identified the south. It is an age in which both men and women work outside the home, usually earn somewhat comparable wages, and share housekeeping chores. When a man chooses a wife, he seeks out someone who is well educated, and prefers to work outside the home. If she happens to earn a six figure salary, so much the better. It is considered fashionable by so-called "power couples" to eat all their meals outside the home, and indeed many of the homes being built today do not have kitchens. The homely craft of sewing, once so necessary, has joined shoe-cobbling as a quaint practice of our ancestors, and the fabric stores of yesterday no longer exist, except in a few rare cases.

When the Great Depression hit, the second of these ages, the industrial age, was in full flower. Almost without exception, the people with whom I attended school had fathers who worked in the mills. In our locality, the parent company of all the mills was the "Tennessee Coal Iron and Land Company", or just "Tennessee Company" as it was called, or TCI for short. They operated numerous coal mines, iron ore mines, blast furnaces, smelters, and a rolling mill, paid the going wage, and offered good health care for their workers.

Our family had followed a different lifestyle. My parents had a certain disdain for people who worked for wages and lived payday to payday, which was about all the wages paid at that time permitted. They called it "living out of a paper sack', meaning, of course, a grocery bag. They wanted to be independent and work for themselves. They didn't believe in debt, and held to the belief that anything you couldn't pay for in cash, you didn't need. Our lifestyle, with our feet still buried in the agricultural age was at first a disadvantage because we had to work very hard doing the field work, and daily chores. Later, however, as the Depression deepened, and most of the industrial jobs ended, we at least never went hungry, as many did, because there was always plenty of plain farm-raised food and plenty of meat. My parents had previously run a dairy. When I was about four years old, they phased out the dairy and went into the chicken and egg business. All through my growing up years, the chicken house stood on the side of the hill above our house, and was about half the size of the house we lived in. It had racks where the chickens could roost at night, safe from predators, and along the wall, there were nests for the hens.   I remember when I was very small helping put some of the chickens in coops to go to market, or sitting for long periods inspecting and packing eggs in large crates, each holding thirty dozen, to go to market.

By the time the Depression came, my father had reinvented himself again, and was now a cattleman. He had bought land in the next county, and grazed his herd there, his herd being about 125 head of cattle. He had a large truck and was usually out with it, buying and selling cattle while my mother and the kids stayed home and kept the place running. We all worked very, very hard.

My earliest memory of the Depression was when my father came home from town and said that the stock market had crashed. My father, product of a backwoods childhood, highly intelligent but poorly educated, thought the "stock" in the stock market meant livestock, such as pigs, cattle, and goats. As it happened, it was all the same to him, a cattleman, for such was his stock in trade. If he couldn't sell a cow, or a side of beef, it was Depression time in his world.

I remember that things went along fairly smoothly for a time. My father worried a lot, and the men of the community were losing their jobs at an increasing rate. About six months after the crash, however, my parents began fighting back in the way they knew best. They set out to weather the storm by becoming self sufficient, in the way their ancestors had when they first came to the wilderness that

3

would one day become the state of Alabama. This was in the spring of the year 1930.

We had always had a kitchen garden, but that year, as the first signs of spring appeared, farming began on a larger scale. I remember that it was a surprise to me when a plowman appeared and began breaking the fields for planting. I hadn't heard it mentioned before, but then my parents never discussed business within hearing of the kids. My parents owned about 600 acres of land, counting the grazing tract. Of that, about 30 acres was put into cultivation, to raise food for the family and the animals, which included several dogs, the milk cows, Nell the horse, hogs, goats, and chickens. We ate corn bread with the noon and evening meals every day of our lives, so it was essential to plant a large tract of corn, not only to be ground into meal for the family, but also to feed the livestock. Then we planted sweet potatoes, peanuts, pole beans (which we planted among the corn to avoid having to build a framework to which they could cling), bunch beans, field peas, large patches of tomatoes, squash, eggplant, okra, onions, sorghum, peanuts, popcorn, watermelons and cantaloupes.

It was all very hard work, and since most of the children were still very young, most of the field work except the plowing and harrowing fell on my older sister, our mother, and me. When I was ten years old, I was doing a man's work. My father was usually out with the truck, trying to make a few dollars to buy the few things we couldn't raise on the farm, such as medicine, school clothes and books, and to pay the doctor and dentist. He also had built a small slaughter house on the place, and furnished some of the markets in town with beef. My mother at this time was still having babies at regular two-year intervals, so was unable to help with the field work much of the time. With all the younger siblings, what little time I had that could have been play time was allotted to baby sitting. Four of my five younger siblings were boys, and young as I was, I found the job overwhelming. I love all my brothers dearly, but at the time, I was much too young to be given such responsibility. However, we were all doing the best we could, especially our parents, so I didn't blame them in any way.

As time went on, we heard of more and more of our neighbors who were "getting surplus". If an industrial worker had been laid off for very long, the family began to experience hunger. Franklin Delano Roosevelt, God rest his soul, was president at the time, and was scrambling for solutions to the suffering. He came up with a plan to pay the farmers in other parts of the country for the products they couldn't sell (the "surplus"), and distribute them to the families who were unable to buy food. The food items that I remember hearing of people receiving were cheese, prunes, flour and lard. Those who did receive these things did so with embarrassment. No one talked about it, but at school we could tell who was receiving surplus by the shoes they wore. The shoes the government distributed as surplus were distressingly plain black leather and very ugly. I was forever thankful that I never had to wear them. Although my sister and I did wear some that were very similar, they were always bought and paid for.

My parents helped many, many people during the Depression. Although we lived remote from any settlement, or even any neighbors, it was not uncommon for a tramp traveling the county road or the railroad to come to our back door and ask for food. My mother never turned anyone away. She usually had something left over from the most recent meal. Cooking for a large family and for the several dogs we always had, she by habit cooked very large amounts, and there was always something left. The convicts who worked the chirt road which ran about a hundred yards down the hill from our house, also came many times, asking to buy peaches and various things, to vary their diet, and they always collectively found enough money to pay the pittance my mother asked. We always felt sorry for them. Most were just hard-scrabble types who had been caught making moonshine and been sent away for a year and a day. There were times when a neighbor would just come to my parents and ask for a bushel of potatoes or corn or whatever. A few times, however, we found where someone had come into our cornfield, shucked and shelled out a bushel of corn, left the shucks and cobs lying, and apparently gone on their way to the grist mill with a sackful of corn over their shoulder. My parents never minded. We could see the hunger all around us, so who could begrudge a bushel of corn?

I remember only one instance in which my mother seemed a bit irritated. Milk was a very important part of our diet, and we usually had three or four milk cows. After they were milked in the morning, they would be turned out into the woods to graze. At about five o'clock in the afternoon someone would go find the cows and drive them to the barn for the evening feeding and milking. One day, my mother went to get the cows and found that they had already been milked. That really irritated my mother, because she thought she knew who had done the deed, and this person was making pots of money in the bootleg trade, protected locally by a crooked sheriff, while our family was digging in the dirt to make an honest living.

Meanwhile, in Washington, President Roosevelt, who at the beginning of his presidency said that fully one third of our country (meaning the south) was poorly clothed, poorly housed and poorly fed, was scrambling to find ways to ease the misery. He was one of the few people who seemed to see, and to care, that the south had never fully recovered from the Civil War, and a large percentage of the people were poor already, and now completely devastated by this new disaster. Working with congress, he enacted the Works Progress Administration, or WPA, which put people to work on municipal projects. They built city halls and other municipal buildings, many of which still stand today, and are considered so stable that they are used as hurricane shelters. Artists were put to work painting murals on the walls. Writers were put to collecting and writing histories of the communities, and laborers were put to building roads. Some of these workers were so weakened by lack of food that they asked for leniency from their bosses until they could draw their first pay check and buy food and thereby get the strength to work. The suffering was indeed great.

Perhaps the most important thing Roosevelt did for young people was to create the Civilian Conservation Corps, or CCC, as it was called. Under this act, young men over the age of 18 could sign up and become part of an organization which, as I remember, was patterned roughly after the army. They wore army-like uniforms (perhaps surplus from World War 1?) and lived in barracks. Their camps, which they built themselves, were located in remote spots in the woods, and were so well built that most of them are still in use today as Boy Scout camps and state park facilities. The men were fed well and were paid a small salary, which they could send home to their families.

Roosevelt created many more "alphabetical agencies", as they were called at the time, People not being accustomed to acronyms, as we are today. He created the Tennessee Valley Authority or TVA, which harnessed the great Tennessee River, built dams and power plants, and made electricity available to all the southeast, and the Rural Electrification Agency, or REA, which brought electricity to rural areas such as ours.

His wife Eleanor was the power behind the creation of the National Youth Administration, or NYA, which furnished money for thousands of young people to get a college education who never would have otherwise. I count myself among them.

I would be remiss if I did not mention the Social Security Administration, which was established under Roosevelt's leadership. Up until this time, there had been no provision for the sustenance of older people. Each family being responsible for their own, the usual scenario was that one of the daughters of the family who had been unable to find a husband stayed home and took care of the parents, ran the farm as best she could, and received her payment later when she inherited the home and farm. However, in the absence of an "old maid" in the family, the parents sometimes merely selected one of the daughters to remain at home and take care of them. It was not a very good plan, and many people suffered extreme poverty and deprivation in their old age. At first, the social security system was very modest. On my very first job, which was selling candy in a five and dime store, I earned a dollar and a half a day, and of that the social security took four cents. However, modest as this suggests they must have been, there can be no doubt that the monthly stipends which the fund later dispensed were a godsend to many older people who then could at least buy food.

Thus the Depression dragged on, year after weary year, sapping the strength of the older people, and robbing the young of their hopes and dreams. If one was negligent and left the laundry hanging on the outside line overnight, it might be stolen. Everyone owned chickens, but they had to be locked securely in the chicken house at night, or they might be stolen. We had several very good watch dogs, so we never suffered any such loss, but once some evidently hungry person came into our house when no one was home and stole several dozen eggs. Another time they stole money. We were so very fortunate, however, in that we fared much better than most. In the following chapters, I shall attempt to tell you of how we lived during this time, and how we endured. That is what people did-- they humbly endured. There was no thought of rioting or looting or any self-defeating "civil disobedience" of the kind we sometimes see today. Most historians think that we didn't really pull out of the Depression until World War II came, and the preparations for defense started the money to flow once again. My memories of this period are very clear, and I agree with the historians. The war was a terrible, terrible time in our history, but at least people were no longer going hungry. Perhaps the greatest end result of the Depression is that it produced what Tom Brokaw has called "the greatest generation". The generation of young people who grew up during the Depression was the same one who in World War II flew the B 24's, the 17's and 29's in the battlefields of Europe and Japan. These pilots were just kids, as were the millions of their comrades who fought and sometimes died in less glamorous jobs. Today these Depression kids are credited with saving the world for democracy. Out of the hard soil of near starvation, deep deprivation and hardship sprang forth a very great generation of Americans.

II

Dog Fennels and China Berry Trees

The house in which my family spent the Depression years was built before I was born. Built by a neighbor who lived on the other side of the ridge, with his son-in-law as his helper, the house was no architectural marvel, but was as good as any other in the vicinity. Built of heart pine (residual from my father's days as a lumberman), and never painted, it had weathered to a grayish color, and to this day has never rotted. The design would probably best be called late dog-trot, with four large, perfectly square rooms, two on either side of a huge enclosed dog-trot hallway, the whole topped by a bonnet roof covered with tar-paper shingles. This design could be seen all over the south at this time, especially in the "company houses" of mill towns and mining camps. The wall, ceilings and floors were all built of "tongue and groove" ceiling cut from heart pine, and had never been painted or adorned in any way. There was only one picture on the walls, and that was a pastel in a large frame with convex glass of my mother's parents which was done the day after they were married. There were no rugs or coverings of any kind on the floors, which had been scrubbed so often with lye soap that they were a light gray color. The windows had no curtains, but in my earliest memories they did have the remnants of window shades which my mother probably had bought when the house was new.

There was only one closet in the house. It was in back bedroom, which served as my parents' bedroom, sitting room for the family, and study room. It was the only room in the house that was ever heated, and usually the only one in which there was a coal oil lamp at night. When the house was new, my father had installed a Delco generator under the high front end, and it would generate electricity for the house and barn. My parents were running a dairy at that time, and lights in the barn were necessary, and lamps would have been very dangerous, considering the clumsiness of farm animals, and the flammability of hay. Hence the Delco. When I was small, we were the only family in the countryside that had electricity. By the time the Depression came, however, the Delco was tired, and soon quit forever. Then we began using coal oil lamps, which are dirty, inefficient, and very difficult to use when there is a large family.

To get back to the closet in the back bedroom, it wasn't much of a closet, only about eight by eight feet, and about half of it was taken up by the chimney. It was used mostly as a place to pile the dirty clothes, waiting for washday. The clothes that we wore from day to day we hung on large nails driven into the walls. Above the closet, next to the chimney, there was a large hole in the ceiling, and as a child, I loved to climb up through the hole and into the loft just to see what was there.

Situated on the sloping south side of Bluff Ridge, a link in the great Appalachian chain, and therefore sitting on an incline, the back of the house rested on the ground, while the front was on pillars (actually lengths of heart pine tree trunks), about five feet high. A porch ran the width of the house in front, and having no banisters up until sometime during the Depression, was very dangerous. My older sister fell over the edge as a child and broke her collar bone. There was no running water and no indoor plumbing, until after we had grown up and had it installed for our parents. Our only heat was from a fireplace in the back bedroom, where my parents slept. Electricity and telephones didn't come until many years later.

Cooking was done on a wood-burning range in the kitchen, with a flue carrying the smoke out through the roof. Cutting stove wood and bringing it in was a daily chore, and the fire had to be fed periodically while a meal was being prepared. Our water had to be brought from a spring located about a quarter mile away, which my great grandfather had scooped out of a hollow when he first came to the area back in 1840. When I was about six years old my parents hired a neighbor to dig a well at the back of the house. He would blast with dynamite and then dig and remove the dirt. One day he didn't get out of the well quite fast enough after igniting the fuse to set off a charge, and the fumes from the blast made him very ill, and they had to pull him out of the well fast, using the rope, bucket, and windlass, which they always used to lower and later retrieve him. After the well was dug, they hired another neighbor to build a thick concrete slab across the back of the house along with a concrete curbing for the well, and the pipes for an indoor sink. What luxury! Then with weather-boarding and screen, and a roof, they enclosed the concrete slab, making a concrete-floored back porch all across the back of the house. There was just one thing wrong. The well had not been dug deep enough and would go dry each summer, and we would have to go back to bringing our water from great grandfather's spring. Correction; two things wrong--the proposed sink was never installed, so from then on forevermore, there was a metal pipe about two inches in diameter and three feet high sticking out of the concrete floor near the well.

Mail delivery in those days was very primitive, by today's standards. We had rural mail delivery, but it didn't quite come to our house. I suppose the route could only come a certain number of miles from town, and the route ended about a quarter mile from our house, and much, much further from the people who lived further up the road. The row of mailboxes, about eight in number, stood on a very lonely stretch of road, with no houses anywhere in the vicinity. During the school year, the school children would pick up the mail on their way home. In the summer, it was a gathering place for the young people from miles up the road, who would come about ten o'clock in the morning, go swimming in the creek which ran beside the road, and wait for the mailman. I remember our box number was 313, which some people today might consider to be an unlucky number, but I don't remember it ever being mentioned in our family. The local superstitions ran more to the fear of a night encounter with a mysterious horseman at Prince Crossing than with numerology. Prince Crossing was where the narrow chirt road crossed the Southern Railroad about three quarters of a mile from our house. My grandfather told the story of meeting a strange night riding horseman there very late one dark night. He was convinced it was a ghostly apparition. As for the mail delivery, it was a very unsatisfactory system. If mail was left in the box any time at all, it was likely to be stolen. Sometime in the middle of the Depression the mail route was extended, and we had a mailbox in front of our house. Our box number then was 488, and so it remained until after WWII

On the grounds surrounding our house, in my earliest memories, there were no flowers. My mother had too much other farm work to do to spend any energy on flowers. Besides, the livestock all roamed free at that time, and any flowers would immediately be devoured by the cows or the goats.

The ground was bare, and was swept occasionally with a brush broom made from branches of the dogwood tree. This was typical of most of the country homes in that area and at that time. Eventually, however, a stock law was passed, and everyone had to keep their livestock within a fenced area. When that happened, residents began to grow beautiful flowers in their yards.

During the Depression my sister and I were old enough to be in home economics classes in school and we tried to improve the grounds surrounding our home. I remember there was a huge red-oak tree in the front yard, very near the porch, which leached all the nutrients from the surrounding soil. My sister managed to get someone to cut the tree down, and we carried rocks and boulders to fill up the ditches and washes, which carried the topsoil down the hill and into the creek with every rain. Then we built up the soil with barnyard fertilizer, of which there was abundance at our farmstead, and planted flowers from seeds and cuttings given to us by neighbors. We painted coffee cans and syrup buckets, filled them with topsoil, and planted houseplants, which we placed along the top of the porch banisters, which had only recently been added to the house. The place became really pretty. We could hear people remarking about it as they passed along the road, and of course my sister and I always made good grades in home economics.

Further away from the house, the dog fennels grew rank, and in midsummer were shoulder high to me. A dog fennel is a tall spidery weed, with foliage resembling that of asparagus. Some people call them summer cedars, and they are not an ugly weed, but quite useless, since nothing will eat them. Bitter weeds were plentiful, also, and when the cows ate them we were unable to drink the milk for a day or two, because of the horrible taste. Butterfly weeds grew all over the ridge and in the summer their orange colored blossoms were a beautiful sight. Today, our beloved butterfly weed has a fancy botanical name, (aselepias tuberosa) and is used as an ingredient in a remedy for nasal and chest congestion. Jemison weeds were also plentiful. Today, these are used as a powerful hallucinogenic drug, but then they were only a nuisance to us, and something the livestock wouldn't eat. Morning glories grew on all the fences, as did maypops (also called passion flowers). In the early morning both were very beautiful. Someone earlier (probably my mother), had planted three China berry trees along the back of the house. During the Depression years they were quite large, and furnished a welcome shade under which we could do the laundry and other chores. In the spring, they were covered with bunches of purplish blooms, and were quite fragrant, but in the fall, they became pest trees. The leaves and stems would fall over the yard, and then the berries. The berries were wooden and had a small hole through the middle like a bead. At times we dyed and strung them for Christmas tree decorations but the result was hardly worth the effort, so we usually swept the berries up with the stems and burned both.

The family laundry, mentioned above, was an all-day job. During the Depression years, our mother was almost always either pregnant or recovering from childbirth, so my older sister and I did the laundry. We had a very large black wash pot in the back yard, which we would fill with water and build a fire beneath it. Then we would shave a large bar of Octagon soap into the water and let it boil, melting the soap. While this was happening, we would run the clothes through the first wash, scrubbing them on the washboard in cold water with Octagon soap. This was to get all the stains out and remove any stubborn soiling. Then the clothes would go into the wash pot and be boiled for about three quarters of an hour, then taken out, leaving the soapsuds in which they had boiled, ready for another load. This process had to be repeated at least three times to accommodate all the laundry that had accumulated during the preceding week. In addition, the fire had to be kept up to keep the wash pot boiling, and the water all had to be drawn from the well or brought from the spring. Then there was the matter of starch. All our school clothes and the boys' blue denim overalls had to be starched stiff. We made the starch with flour and boiling water, and dipped each garment before hanging them on the long clotheslines, which stretched three times between the large red oak trees on the side of the hill above our kitchen. It was a hard day's work, doing the washing for our large family. In the wintertime, the whole process would be moved into the screened-in back porch. Then when the clothes were hung on the line, if the weather was really cold, they would freeze stiff, and might stay that way for days.

Before we go any further, let me tell you about Octagon soap, briefly mentioned earlier. Octagon soap was a brown soap made by the Colgate Palmolive Company, and was the cheapest soap on the market during the Depression. It kept clean an entire generation of Depression-ridden southerners. Similar to the lye soap our pioneer ancestors had made using ashes and hog lard, it was an excellent cleaner, and even seemed to have some healing properties. We used it not only for the laundry, but for washing dishes, scrubbing the floors, washing our hair, bathing, cleaning wounds, and any other task where a reliable cleaner was needed. Some years ago, I found Octagon soap still being sold in an A&P store in Atlanta. I have a bar which I keep just to remind myself how lucky we all are to have the things we need, and how wonderful it is just to see people who work hard do well. I also appreciate not having to wonder if behind their brave demeanor a hungry stomach may be their daily companion.

When the laundry was finished, there was the ironing to be done. Not having any electricity, the ironing had to be done with flat irons, which we heated on the cook stove or in the fireplace. It was hard to keep from getting ashes on the iron and then onto whatever you were ironing. Sometimes in the summertime, after we were finished with the wash we would heat the irons in the coals from the wash pot fire and do the ironing in the backyard under the china berry trees. I really hated ironing, especially the boy's overalls. Denim is such a heavy material to begin with, and when it is new and starched really stiff, it can be very difficult to iron. Still a child at the time, I found it to be an almost impossible task, but it was something that was part of my job, so I did it. The many good years since that time have not dimmed my memory of some facets of those difficult years.

The woods surrounding our homestead were beautiful. In the spring they were white with dogwoods, yellow with Jasmine, and pink with crabapple trees and honeysuckles in full bloom. The ground would be a colorful quilt of anemones, wild pansies (called rooster heads), sweet Williams, and trailing arbutus. There was not a great deal of undergrowth, as there is today, and walking in the woods was a favorite pastime. Today, the flowers are mostly gone. The creek, which ran in front of our house, about fifty yards down the hill, was wide, free flowing and unspoiled. Later on, some hillbilly bootlegger types built a shotgun house on a bluff overlooking the creek, about a mile upstream from us. This was our first experience with real white trash. Instead of burning their garbage, or burying it in a stump hole as other people did, they merely tossed it out the back door, down the bluff and into the creek. Soon the creek was unusable for swimming, fishing, or, as a few times became necessary, washing clothes. Littered with old tires, broken fruit jars, and the general detritus of hillbilly living, it soon became a sad reminder of the beautiful stream it had been.

Across the field in front of our house, and beyond the creek and the chirt road, there was a railroad. It always ran two passenger trains a day, the morning train, and the evening train. Then, as I remember, there was about four freight trains, some of which were very, very long. They carried coal, crude oil, cattle, saw logs, pulp wood, and farm products. Often, the really long trains would have trouble climbing the mountain about a mile up the track, but they always made it one way or the other. There was no sidetrack anywhere nearby where they could uncouple a few of the cars and pick them up later. The trains were like neighbors to us. The engineers and flagmen would wave to us as we worked in the field, and seemed to be very nice people.

Just before the Depression descended on us, my father had bought some property in the next county, and grazed his cattle there. Sometimes the cattle would get onto one of the tracks that ran through that county. These were different railroad lines from the one that ran in front of our homestead. Even though it was miles away, my father would always hear the train whistle and know some of the cattle were on the track. He tried to keep them away from the tracks as much as possible. He always had bells on several of the animals in any particular group, with a distinctive sounding bell on the lead cow. By listening for the bells, even from a great distance, my father could discern the approximate location of the group and know if they were near the tracks. When they did stray onto the tracks, the engineers had a certain way of blowing the whistle, and my father would immediately get in his truck and go. He could always tell the approximate location, from the sound of the whistle. Sometimes the cattle would have been hit by the train and have broken legs, and he would have to shoot them, and this always broke my heart. Even though I was only a child, it was always my job to write to the railroad companies and tell them of the loss, which the engineer would have already reported, and the companies always paid. The railroads were always good corporate neighbors.

Another company that was always fair in their dealing with us was the Southern Natural Gas Company. During the Depression they installed a pipeline from Texas to Georgia. It cut across about ninety acres of our property and just touched the corner of our yard. They took a right of way about forty feet across, as I remember, but they paid a fair price for it, and the money was a godsend to our family. I remember the ditcher they brought in, and the huge pipes they buried in the ground. One of my male cousins was living with us at the time and helping with the farm work, as he had been unable to find other work. When the pipeline came through, he saw it as a good opportunity to get a job, so he asked, and they hired him. He stayed with the crew all the way into Georgia, "batching" in trailers along the right of way. Since then, the Southern Natural Gas Company sends out a plane each Christmas to drop a bag of goodies at each homestead along the route. They really go all out trying to be a good neighbor.

One thing that became a common sight on the roads of the southland during the Depression was the Hoover wagon. Few people had the money to buy a car, and the ones they had owned before hard times struck eventually wore out. When their car became so dilapidated that it could no longer be fixed, the owner quite often would remove the top and the engine, hitch the mule to it and away they would go in their "Hoover wagon". It was one of the weirdest sights I have ever seen. However, it was one way of getting where you wanted to go, and buying hay was cheaper than buying gas. However, no one we knew ever ate "Hoover hogs". A Hoover hog is an Armadillo, and I understand that people in Florida and states west of us ate Hoover hogs during the Depression. The reason we didn't, no doubt, was because Armadillos are not found in the area where we lived.

Thus, you have a general picture of the surroundings in which we lived during the Depression. It was really hard scrabble, but most southerners with their Celtic backgrounds have a highly developed sense of humor. This sense of humor stood us in good stead during these difficult times. If one had nothing to eat except butterbeans and cornbread, one made that acceptable by laughing at the situation. Likewise, if one was wearing
trousers that were full of holes, his friends might kiddingly ask him if he killed that dog, (meaning the imaginary one that supposedly attacked him and tore his trousers). This was their way of dealing with the fact of their desperate poverty. There were many jokes about the high carbohydrate, flatulence-producing foods that everyone ate. Sweet potatoes and prunes were the worst offenders, and butterbeans, the main staple of most diets, ran a close second

III

Cornbread, Butterbeans, Catfish, and Poke Salad

During the decade known as The Great Depression our family raised most of the food we ate. Very little came from Piggly Wiggly, the store where my father traded in town, seven miles away. Besides the huge fields of corn, black-eyed peas, sweet potatoes and sorghum, we always had a large kitchen garden in which we raised tomatoes, eggplant, English peas, lettuce, onions, okra, peppers, radishes, squash, cabbage, speckled butterbeans, and always a turnip patch. Turnips are one thing that will grow winter or summer, and in the winter we would also have a collard patch alongside the turnips.

When we sat down to a meal, we thought we were eating "poor do", as it was called, but I suppose we ate a much healthier diet than most people do today. My father always butchered, so we always had beef plus chicken, turkey, and wild game from the surrounding woods. In the fall we would have a hog butchering, and the entire family would have to help. My father always did the actual killing with a .22 caliber rifle. Then we would lift the carcasses one by one and douse them in a barrel, which we had filled with boiling water. A few seconds in the barrel, and the bristles would detach from the skin fairly easily. After removing the bristles my father would gut the carcass, salvage the heart, liver and sometimes the intestines. We never, but never ate chitterlings, but my father had a doctor friend in Bessemer who was especially fond of chitterlings as well as mountain oysters (don't ask) so we disposed of them by sending them to the doctor.

We always did the hog butchering in the evening, just after dark, and after ward, my father would hoist the carcasses on pulleys and let then hang overnight to chill in the night air. Next day, there would be more work to be done, "working up" the meat as it was called. It had to be cut into usable pieces and in the early days usually salted. In later times, after electricity came, we had a large deep freeze. The hardest part was making the sausage and rendering the lard. My father would cut the carcass into pieces. Then he and my mother would trim all the fat off, cut it into small pieces and collect it in a pile. Then the lean parts, and this included the hams cut into small pieces, would go into another pile.

At that point we were ready to grind sausage. We had a hand-operated sausage grinder that my parents had had forever, which we bolted to one side of the cook table in the kitchen. Then one person would feed the machine while another ground and a third mixed salt and sage into the ground meat on the other end. This really was a family affair, and each would take their turn at the grinding, which was the hardest part. Then the canning would begin. We always canned all the sausage, even in later years, when we had a huge freezer chest. The chest was usually full of vegetables, so we still canned the sausage. It had to be canned before spoilage had a chance to set in, so many times my mother would stay up all night, canning sausage. After that, the lard had to be rendered. For this, my mother would bring the large wash pot into the house, put it in the fireplace, build a fire under it, and fill it with the fat we had trimmed from the pork. The fireplace was large, but the wash pot was also large, and was a tight fit, but she rendered lard in that fashion for years without ever an accident, however, she always made sure she had the rendering done and the wash pot out of the fireplace before the kids came home from school. Cooking the fat for several hours until the lard had cooked out of it, it was then dipped out into fifty-pound cans and ten-pound buckets and allowed to cool. This would be enough lard to last until next hog-killing time. We always used nothing but pure lard back then, but we always worked so hard, no one ever had any ill effects from it. The "cracklings" that were left after the lard was rendered, we used in cornbread instead of lard, and let me tell you, crackling cornbread is really good.

We also ate goat from time to time. We never ate lamb, not because we had any prohibitions concerning it, but just that no one in the area raised sheep. When I was growing up, if one said, "barbecue", it meant goat. I never even heard of barbecued beef or pork until many years later. However, barbecued goat meat is very good. We would put an entire carcass on the grill; let it cook all night over the coals of an oak fire, basted from time to time with a sweet and sour sauce. Someone in the family would be designated to tend the fire and keep the meat turning and basted. This usually was in preparation for a celebration of some kind, a wedding anniversary, family reunion or the Fourth of July.

When my father butchered, there were certain parts of the beef that didn't sell well in town, and we ate those. We often had ox tail soup. My mother would cut the tail into joints, boil it for a few hours, then add as many vegetables as were to be found in the garden at that time or a jar of "soup mix" (usually tomatoes, corn, okra, and peppers) from last summer's canning. To come home from school to a hot bowl of such soup and cornbread to go with it was pretty close to heaven. Sometimes, in the absence of soup, she would have a large pan of baked sweet potatoes, which were handy, since we could put a potato in our pocket and go about our chores, and get finished a bit sooner than if we had taken time to eat.

Another thing that didn't sell well in town was the head, anything except the brains. My mother would open the skull with a hatchet and extract the brains. These we only ate occasionally, when they didn't sell, but the jowls and the tongue we always ate. My mother would trim the meat from the jowls, and there was always quite a lot of it, and make hash. It was really good. The tongues she would boil and slice, and that was also very tasty. We also always ate the beef hearts. If it had been a young beef, she would slice and fry it. If it was a larger heart, it would be stuffed and roasted as you would roast a turkey. I remember that it was delicious. We also from time to time ate tripe. This would be boiled until it was tender, then battered and fried, and it was quite tasty.

Fried chicken for breakfast was a special treat, with hot biscuits and saw mill gravy. My mother always made her biscuits in a large bread pan that had been carved from a length of log. For rolling pie crusts, she used a rolling pin that had been carved in the same manner, from the branch of a tree. If my father had butchered the night before, we might also have fried beef liver, beef heart, beef brains scrambled with eggs, or fried pork chops. Quite often we would have what was called "white meat", which was the side meat of the hog (sow belly), that had been salted down to preserve it.

This would usually be sliced, soaked in buttermilk overnight, and fried for breakfast. With the ubiquitous buttermilk biscuits and saw mill gravy, sorghum syrup and butter, it made a very good meal. Quite often for breakfast, we would have just fried potatoes, which we loved, or my mother would boil a box of raisins and we would have just potatoes or just raisins, with biscuits, butter, home made jelly, jam, or preserves, and always sorghum syrup and plenty of milk. I can also remember eating fried corn for breakfast, and loving it. We always had several milk cows, so there was never a shortage of milk and butter. Sometimes for the first meal of the day we would have toasted cheese. My mother would slice the cheese onto the individual plates and put the plates in the oven for a few minutes. We also sometimes ate eggs for breakfast, along with our white meat. There was always a large flock of chickens in the yard, so there was no shortage of eggs. We always ate well for the time. Many people with large families got by on just biscuits and gravy or rice and gravy for breakfast, and sometimes all three meals, day after day, for years.

We also at that time ate things from the surrounding woods. We often had batter fried squirrel for breakfast. One of my mother's brothers was a very skilled woodsman, having learned it from his grandfather who learned it from the Indians. When he was at our house, which was a good part of the time, he would often arise very early, before the rest of us, take the rifle and pop a couple of squirrels out of the treetops, skin and gut them, and have them ready for my mother to cook when she arose. Squirrel was a real treat for us back then, but I wouldn't touch it now, for a myriad of reasons. From time to time we ate 'possum. 'Possum is a very gamey meat, but my mother would roast it surrounded with sweet potatoes, and it was good. I remember once we even ate a large turtle, in the form of turtle stew. I have heard it said that a turtle carcass contains seven different kinds of meat. However, I don't remember any such exotica. I only remember that the stew was very tasty. Our family was inordinately lucky in that our mother was known for her cooking skills. In the spring we would have huckleberry pies, and in midsummer, a blackberry pot pie almost every day. We never got tired of the wild berry pies.

Our noonday meal was the heaviest meal of the day, and we called it dinner. In the summertime we ate many vegetable dinners with cornbread, and sometimes we had meat. Not having a refrigerator, or even an icebox, it was difficult to keep meat from spoiling in the summertime. In the winter, we ate legumes, usually butterbeans, but sometimes black eyed peas, speckled beans, or navy beans, and we usually had meat of some kind, even if it was just a bit of ham cooked with the beans. We always had cornbread, and of course, there was always plenty of milk and butter. If you happened to be anywhere within a hundred yards of a neighbor's house at midmorning, it was not uncommon to hear the clatter of dry beans being dropped into the cooking pot. It was a source of amusement. It is no wonder that southerners have such a highly developed sense of humor. For much of our history, we have had to laugh at ourselves or die.

The evening meal was never any big deal at our house. We all had chores to do, and sometimes were late getting finished, so we ate whenever we could, and usually it was just whatever was left from dinner. My favorite evening meal was cornbread crumbled into a glass of buttermilk. I thought that was really good.

One drink that I really liked was sassafras tea. At that time, sassafras bushes grew thick in the woods near our home. I would dig the roots, wash them and let them dry for a day or two. Then boiling them for a half hour or so, would produce a very tasty tea, the flavor of which closely resembled that of root beer. I understand that in Louisiana, the leaves of the sassafras bushes are dried and pulverized into "file", used in making file gumbo, but we never used anything but the roots.

We rarely ate fish. Not living near any large body of water, seafood in any quantity was not readily available. Our palates were never trained in that category of comestibles, so we weren't aware of missing anything. We fished in Rice Creek, and ate the catfish we caught and occasionally my father would bring home red snapper from the market in town. We ate more canned red salmon than any other fish. My mother would scramble it with eggs and onions, and with the bones left in. We weren't aware of it then, but we were getting extra calcium that way. My mother was far ahead of her time when it came to nutrition. She was part Cherokee, and I think such knowledge was intuitive with her.

Some people ate 'coon (raccoon) during the Depression, but we never did. 'Coons are such friendly little animals, I suppose our family would rather have gone hungry, if we had to, than eat one. Other plant-based things in our diet that came from the woods besides blackberries and huckleberries were black haws, wild plums, persimmons, hickory nuts and scaly barks, paw paws, maypops, and poke salad. Our family was especially fond of poke salad. Poke salad is a humble weed that grows everywhere in the southland. Gathered in the very early spring, the young shoots are very tasty when boiled, then stir fried with eggs and onions and eaten with corn bread. I still eat poke salad whenever I can. I have seen it growing along the roadsides and fencerows all over the eastern United States and the Midwest, but I don't think it has ever been considered fit for human consumption anywhere except in the south. Following the Civil War, when the northerners had stolen or destroyed all the foodstuffs stored in southern barns and smokehouses, many southerners would have starved had it not been for poke salad. Most had no ammunition with which to hunt game, or seeds to plant a garden, the destruction had been so complete. Even the mature stalks of poke salad can be eaten. In the late summer when the stalks have reached a height of about five feet and produced berries, some enthusiasts cut the stalks, peel them, and cut the core into pieces. These are then battered and fried in the same way that one would fry okra.

One other thing that we ate during the Depression, as mentioned above and that I have always been especially fond of is wild persimmons. My father always loved to tell the story of when I was about three years old (this would have been a few years before the Depression came) I got my hands on a bucketful of persimmons that someone had gathered. Sitting down on the front steps, I ate every one, but on reaching the bottom of the bucket, I ran into one or two that were not entirely ripe. (As anyone who has ever eaten wild persimmons knows, if one is not entirely ripe, it will pucker you mouth like alum). At that point, and after eating a bucketful of them, I threw the bucket away from me and said, "Oooo, I don't like old 'immons". My father never let me live that down. Looking back, I am sure that the "bucket" was a small half gallon syrup bucket, not a bigger full gallon syrup or lard bucket. Even I could not have eaten that many.

Entertaining during the Depression was very different from what most of us have become accustomed to in more recent times. Everyone who had fruit trees and a garden canned fruits and vegetables in the summertime, to use in the winter. Our family usually canned 500 jars every summer, and most of them were half gallons. Nothing was ever less than a quart, even jams, jellies, or preserves. The one thing that most people always had or could get was canned peaches, and most people could manage to get the ingredients for a simple layer cake. Therefore, when one attended a social function of any kind, and this included church functions, showers, or parties of any description, the refreshments served always consisted of a slice of cake on a small plate, and some slices of canned peaches beside it, with nothing to drink. We had often walked long distances to get to the social function, and faced another long walk home, so the cake and peaches always tasted good to us, however quaint it all seems today.

We lived as one with the woods, the fields, and nature. At night, the surrounding woods were often alive with foxhunters who had come out from town. There was one I remember in particular, a bank president, who had a large pack of beagles, and would run them in our woods at least once a week. Late at night, if there were no dogs in the woods, we might hear a fox bark. No one in our family ever did any night hunting that I remember, but we often fished at night. As the boys grew older they would often go frog gigging at night. (If you haven't eaten frog legs, you have a treat waiting). We were as nearly self sufficient as I think anyone could have been at the time. The few things we did buy were bought in large quantities to save money. Sugar and salt were always bought in one hundred pound bags, and flour was bought by the barrel. It didn't really come in a barrel, but in twelve twenty-pound bags.

I have heard people say that they grew up poor but never realized they were poor. I can't say that. We weren't really poor. My father was wealthy in land and cattle, but we were poor in that there often was no money for clothes or for the everyday things like sliced bread for school lunches. Also, our family kept getting larger, and by the time the Depression was in mid term, my mother had had two more children, and taking care of our family involved not only a great deal of work, but of necessity a certain amount of money. Yes, from a monetary standpoint, we were poor, and I felt it every day of my life. Pride runs very deep in our family, and I suppose I have my share of it. The entire Depression experience and the perceived indignities of it battered my pride. Today, I have had more life experience, and wouldn't mind at all taking biscuits in my lunch, for instance, but back then it dealt a mortal blow to my self esteem.

IV

Rags, Tags and Cow Chow Bags

As has been indicated in the previous chapter, our family ate well during the Depression compared to other families. Granted it was plain food, but there was always plenty for our large family and for any stranger who happened to drop by. Clothes and household linens, however, were a different matter. There was seldom any money for clothes. My mother had always made everything that she and my sister and I wore, plus the boys' shirts and everything the younger children wore, but during the Depression my sister had begun making her own clothes, and at age thirteen I began making my own. At the time, good cotton cloth was fifteen cents a yard, but cloth of a lesser quality sold for ten cents a yard. The trouble was, no one had the few pennies it took to buy enough material for a dress. During the summer, my sister and I would pick wild blackberries and send them to town to be sold for ten cents a gallon. Picking blackberries is very difficult work, considering the intense heat in midsummer when the blackberries are ripe, the snakes that are likely to live in a blackberry patch, and the thorns that scratch the picker from fingertips to elbow. Ten cents is very poor pay for a gallon of blackberrie s, but we were glad to get it. I remember once we picked sixteen gallons. Before school started each year, we would try to get enough money to buy enough material for two or three cotton dresses, which would have to do for the school year. Each day when we came home from school and before we did the afternoon chores, we would have to change our clothes and keep them clean to wear again. That way, the two or three dresses that we had could be made to last until washday, whenever that was. We always wore our clothes until they were rags, and then the rags were used for bathing, for dishcloths or for scrubbing and cleaning. Blue denim overalls were selling for as little as fifty cents a pair at the time, but the boys wore theirs until they were full of ho les and my mother would patch them with scraps from other worn-out overalls and ravelings from feed sacks. I don't know how she ever sewed with the thick thread (almost cord) that we called ravelings. It was the coarse thread that was used to make the sacks that feed came in. My mother was a very resourceful woman. When the boys' overalls were so worn they couldn't be patched any more, she would cut them into pieces and make quilts. These were extremely heavy and very warm. I don't know how she ever quilted through the bulkiness of such a thick quilt.

We usually got one pair of shoes a year, and during the summer we went barefoot, except for church. Up until I was in the seventh grade we had to walk a mile and a half to school on a chirt road. Chirt will cut leather and wear shoes out very quickly, so the shoes would always have to be repaired during the year. During the depth of the Depression my father found a place where he could buy Red Goose shoes (a very good brand at the time), for one dollar a pair. The only thing was, they must have been the bottom of the Red Goose line, for they were in a very plain style, and looked exactly like the shoes that the poor people got from surplus. I was so ashamed to wear them I could have died, but my sister would shine hers as if they were the very best, and never indicated that she minded wearing them. In the years since, however, I have found out that she was as mortified as I was, but evidently handled it a bit better. We still talk about those horrible, horrible shoes.

I remember once I did get a nice pair of shoes. My feet must have been "on the ground", as people would say, because my father bought the shoes in town that day and brought them back by the school. As it happened, it was lunch period and everyone was out on the school grounds. There he found my sister, gave the shoes to her, and told her to find me and let me try them on. After she found me, we sat down on the wide front steps of the old white two-room schoolhouse very privately, thank goodness, because everyone was in another part of the school yard.

There, I tried the shoes on. They were beautiful and just what I had wanted for so long. They were high tops, with a row of buttons down the side of each shoe. The tops were grey kid, and the feet were black patent leather. A more beautiful pair of shoes I never hoped to see. They were tight on my feet, but afraid to let them go, I told my sister they fit just fine, and satisfied that she had done as was expected of her, she went back to her classmates. I wore the shoes the rest of that day, on the long walk hone, and for the remainder of that winter, and I have suffered for it ever since. By the time the winter was over, I had huge corns on my toes, and they are still my daily companions, constantly reminding me of that beautiful pair of shoes from hell.

During the Depression, different kinds of "hard times" outfits became fashionable. One summer, dishrag blouses were all the rage. A dishcloth of very loose mesh cost ten cents at the time, and a blouse required four--one for the front, another for the back and one for each sleeve. The waistline and sleeves were drawn into a blouse effect by drawstrings made from flour sack ravelings. My sister and I picked blackberries and got enough dimes to buy four dishrags each and made our blouses. Today it is difficult to believe that we ever wore dishrags, but at the time, we strutted in our dishrags and were thankful to have them.

Jewelry also manifested some strange incarnations during those years. Lapel pins made of yarn flowers became very popular, as did necklaces made of cellophane and paper folded and linked in the manner of a St. Bridgett's cross. Tableware jewelry was another fad. At that time all of the restaurants used silver plated flatware. People in town who had enough money to go to a nice restaurant (This didn't include us country people) might leave with a "souvenir"--perhaps an ice-tea spoon--which would be bent and made into a bracelet. People wore a lot of really tacky things in their struggle to triumph over the drabness of their lives. Wedding jewelry was very plain. Most brides wore just a wedding band, which was a very narrow band of gold. If the couple were more affluent, the band might be platinum, but never anything ostentatious.

No one at this time wore expensive jewelry. Most people simply couldn't afford it, and those who had such things left over from better days didn't wear it because they didn't have the clothes to complement it, or because they didn't want to flaunt their jewelry when other people were having such a hard time. Others had hocked their jewelry, and I heard one dentist's wife say that her husband had melted hers down for the gold to make crowns for his patients' teeth.

Where household linens and some items of clothing were concerned, our family was very fortunate in one way. My father was constantly buying feed for the milk cows, the beef cattle, the horse, chickens, and hogs. And it all came in fabric bags. Then there was the flour, sugar, and salt, which he bought for the household, which also come in fabric bags, all made by the Fulton Bag and Cotton Company, located in Cabbagetown, an old section of Atlanta, Georgia. The story went that a train had once derailed there, and one of the wrecked boxcars had been loaded with cabbage. The surrounding households were allowed to help themselves, and so for some time everyone was eating cabbage, and the place earned the name of Cabbagetown. The owners and managers of Fulton Bag must have had a soft spot in their hearts for the besieged Depression era housewives, or perhaps it was the millers who used their bags who pushed them into it; in any event, they began making their bags of printed cotton material, which when washed made excellent material for home sewing. The prints were really pretty, and everyone envied us because we had an almost unlimited supply of feed sacks. Sugar, salt and flour came in white sacks, but the salt sacks had stripes woven into the fabric and made beautiful dish towels. The sugar sacks were used for bath towels and sheets. My mother would sew several of the sacks together to make a sheet, and none of us ever thought there was anything unpleasant about sleeping on sheets with seams in them. Too many other problems were bigger and more important. The flour sacks were thin and were usually used to make handkerchiefs or underwear. We made all the underwear for the family. Our pride and joy, however, was the pretty feed sacks that cow chow (for the milk cows), shorts (for the hogs), cotton-seed meal (for the cows and horse) and the various other animal feeds came in. Besides dresses, we made pillow slips, curtains, pajamas, and countless other things for ourselves and the household. The sewing machine got a real workout. I had been reluctant to wear feed sacks while in high school. When I was in college however, I wore them, and found that outside of the environment in which I grew up, no one knew the difference.

The coarse, heavy cotton thread that the sacks were sewn with was zealously saved when the sacks were unraveled and washed. At any one time my mother would have a large ball maybe five inches in diameter of these ravelings. She used them for quilting, and the rest of the family went to the ball anytime anyone needed a bit of twine for anything from a bent-pin fishing line to wrapping a package.

There was never any money for warm coats, caps and gloves for the long walk to school, so we made do with whatever we had. I remember my mother sent off to a mail order company and ordered a coat for me when I was in the second grade. I suppose she wanted it to last for a while, so she ordered it large. It almost swept the ground, and I was so ashamed to wear it, but it did keep my legs warm. This was a time when girls' dresses and coats came to just above their knees. I eventually outgrew it, but kept wearing it. That was the last coat I had until I was in high school. My mother would never let me leave home for the long walk to school without something to keep my head warm, and the only "something" I had was a toboggan cap, just a plain woolen stocking cap, of the type that no one but ice hockey players wore at the time. I was the only kid in school who wore one, and I felt ashamed, but on the other hand, and probably as a result, I have never suffered a great deal from ear infections in the years since. I always wore long cotton knit stockings held up by home-made elastic garters just above the knees. Next to my body I wore home-made bloomers made from feed sacks, the bloomers held up by a bodice, which they buttoned onto. They kept me warm, but had little else to recommend them.

Even so, there were so many people who were so much worse off than our family. People all around us didn't have enough to eat, and as has been indicated, we were singularly lucky on that score. Our father was a very hard worker and a good manager, so whatever privations we suffered were not because of any failure on his part, and my mother certainly did her part to hold things together. It was just the times, and the times were as bad as they could get.

My mother spent nothing on herself. In fact, she very rarely went to town. My parents lived according to the ancient code whereby the woman stayed home while the man went to town and did the business for the family. My father managed his money as his pioneer ancestors had for hundreds of years. He had no bank account, having lost money in a bank failure at the beginning of the Depression. He usually carried every penny he had in the world in his pants pocket. I remember once he lost a roll of money, probably by dragging it out of his pocket with something else. He had been with a friend that day, and always thought that the friend had picked it up and kept it. It was only about thirty dollars, as I remember, but at the time thirty dollars would feed a large family for a month. From this incident, I learned very early that friendship can sometimes go out the window when money is involved.

A story that my oldest brother tells illustrates just how scarce money was in our family during the Depression years. This was after my sister was married, which would put it toward the end of the Depression. My brother's class was going on an "end of school" trip to a park some miles away. He had not a penny of money with which to buy his lunch or anything else he might want. My sister happened to be there, and even though my brother-in-law was not a big wage earner at the time, she came and put two dimes in my brother's hand. With most of what we call fast food items selling at a nickel apiece, he said he ate all day on those two dimes. I remember also that my sister and her husband in the early years of their marriage lived on five dollars a week grocery money for many years. It all seems unreal now.

Anything my mother needed she would tell my father and he would get it in town. No one ever made a list, since he couldn't read, and how he remembered everything is a puzzle. Where the problems came was when it came to things we needed at school. I remember once when I was in the second grade and it was Valentine's Day. The teacher hadn't said a word about exchanging valentines, or I could have made some home made ones. Neither had we exchanged valentines in the first grade, so I wasn't expecting it. Then that day just out of the blue, she said, "you can exchange valentines now". It was a complete surprise to me. The students got up from their seats and began going to the desks of other students and delivering their valentines. Not one person gave me a valentine. I put my head down under my desk top and pretended to be looking for something so no one would see that I was crying. Years later I asked my mother why she allowed such things to happen. She said it was because she never got to go to town and had to depend on our father, and he, not being able to read, was no good at buying anything but the most basic things. Truth be told, I doubt that my mother, staying home as she did, was even aware that Valentine's Day was approaching. Anyway, time staggered on, and we endured, year after soul-destroying year, never daring to hope that it would ever be any other way.

V

Stump Jumpers, Puddle Hoppers, and Moon Fixers

This chapter is about the people who lived in the country surrounding us as we were growing up during the Depression. Most of them would be considered eccentrics by today's standards. Some of them were good people, really salt of the earth; others might be described as unreconstructed southerners; not to be trusted very far. Many of them were bootleggers, and once one of these shot and killed one of our milk cows that got into his mash pot. Their children, also, were the terror of the countryside. In some cases, however, the bootleggers were good enough neighbors, just hard luck people trying to survive any way they could. They didn't bother us, and we didn't bother them. Some were protected by the local sheriff, which caused some resentment. Every month we would see the sheriff's car going out our road on his way to get his payoff from certain of them. Seeing this while we were working very, very hard, trying to make an honest living, who could blame us?

These hard-luck types, with their famous southern sense of humor, had some colorful names for each other. An especially tall man was called a "moon fixer". A cross-eyed person was called "tangle eye". A person who wasn't very smart was called "crack bean", and the population in general were "stump jumpers", "puddle hoppers", or "scatology kickers". Instead of "scatology" they used the four-letter word that means the same thing. They joked about the worn and patched clothing they wore, the rough food they ate and the resultant flatulence that did wheelies in their gastrointestinal tracts. California prunes, which the government distributed to the needy, and sweet potatoes, which were raised in hillside garden patches, being the worst offenders were called "music roots", and "whistle berries" respectively.

There was also a very dark side to life. Prohibition was the law of the land at that time, and was the progenitor of more evil than most people could imagine. In the big cities, the so-called underworld came into being, starting with bootlegging whiskey from Canada.

In the backwoods where we lived, there was a more localized version of the same thing. It was a well known fact that many people made and sold bootleg whiskey, which was called "moonshine", or just "shine", "white lightning", "mountain dew", "rotgut", "popskull" and various other colorful names. Their stills were located in the hollows where there was water, and if you did any walking in the woods, you were likely to run across one. Our family had a policy of minding our own business, and we never had any trouble with the bootleggers. They tore up and down the chirt road in front of our house in their souped-up rattletraps, on their way to make their deliveries. Some of them had "cut-outs" on their cars. I'm not sure just what a "cut-out" is, but they made loud, birdlike noises that could be heard for miles in the clear country air. I'm sure it would be illegal today. There were sometimes shootings when the bootleggers would get "likkered up". Once a fellow researcher and I were counting the murders that occurred during those years in that locality, and we counted twelve very easily. People were troubled, and whiskey and trouble don't make a very good mix, especially the mind-altering popskull that was brewed in the hollows roundabout.

Intolerance was the order of the day. Italians and Jews and of course blacks, were the subjects of many jokes and ribald humor. Several times during my school years, the high school presented a minstrel show. Minstrel shows were very popular at the time, and always featured blackface comedians. This was very different from when my mother was growing up in the same place. Their closest neighbor and one of their best friends was a black woman who lived nearby. She had been born a slave on a Georgia plantation belonging to one of my mother's distant relatives. As for the Italians and Jews, their speech patterns were imitated and made the butt of many jokes. It was the accepted way of things, and no one thought anything of it. However, in our family, we were taught compassion and understanding. Thank goodness for that. I remember my mother always spoke with kindness of the Indians, who had also suffered greatly at the hands of white people, and the blacks, who at the time were suffering along with the whites, but to a much greater degree. We were never taught hatred or intolerance.

One source of conflicted thinking among us kids concerned self defense and protecting ourselves against the bullies at school and even worse bullies with whom we were unfortunate enough to have to share the road on the long walk from school. Our mother always taught us to be non-combative, to Biblically turn the other cheek, or to simply walk away. As it happened, none of that worked with these bullies. Our father, on the other hand, who was a strict disciplinarian, would, when he was admonishing me, always say, among other things, "you never take up for yourself coming home from school". I never knew what to do. The one thing I did know was that if I had tried to defend myself from the bullies, they probably would have given me a real beating, not necessarily right then, but sometime when I wasn't expecting it. These kids, coming from a hard-scrabble background, were really mean.

Back then, everyone was a gossip. Today, most people consider themselves above such a useless and sometimes destructive pursuit. At that time, however, first of all, the women all stayed home, kept house, and took care of the family. Having very little outlet for their social inclinations and a very limited world view, the women tended to gossip about their neighbors when they did have someone with whom to talk. Also, because of lack of money, both men and women were denied the pleasure of even a movie now and then, and of course, there was no television. Therefore they gossiped. Most especially, if you happened to be a young person, your activities were closely watched, and if there were no known facts of a salacious nature, someone was sure to make some up. These are harsh words, I realize, but those were harsh times, and sometimes harsh times bring out the harshness in human nature.

Tramps and hobos were a common sight in those days. We lived perhaps a hundred yards from the only road in the area, and about three hundred yards from the Southern railway, both of which had their share of wayfarers and wanderers, all of them hungry. We always grew a large field of corn between the road and the railroad, the yard was always full of chickens, and many other signs of a fairly successful farm operation were visible from the road. Consequently, we were often visited by the hungry travelers walking along the road or the railroad, who probably saw us as a chance to get a good meal. They were always very polite and humble, just hungry people trying to make i to somewhere. We never had any trouble with them, and my mother never turned anyone away. She always cooked more than was necessary for our family because we always had several dogs to feed, and she allowed for them. So there was always something she could put together that probably seemed a feast to a hungry traveler.

Another common sight in the rural south during the Depression was the traveling salesmen. There were several in our area, but two I remember clearly because my mother bought from them consistently. One was the "Watkins man", as we called him, who sold a variety of products, including home remedies such as Cloverine salve and arthritis liniment. Then there was the Jewel Tea Man, whose offerings were mostly coffee and tea, flavorings and spices, and who gave dishes as premiums to those who purchased a certain amount. Those dishes are now prized by collectors. The salesmen would usually sit and talk for a while and show all their products, although they usually knew a big sale would not be their reward. There is little place in today's world for door to door salesmen, but in that time and place, they were a godsend to the lonely housewives, both for the social contact they provided, and the chance to shop without the trip to town.

Mixed in with the stump jumpers, puddle hoppers, and bootleggers that we grew up among; there were also some good and kindly people. I remember an incident that happened when I was in the third grade, the same year the Depression started. It was Christmas time, and the girls in my class at school had made clothes for a doll, which we planned to give to charity. In the course of the sewing and handling by so many little girls, the doll's wrap had become a bit grubby. The teacher asked if someone in the class could take it home, launder it, and bring it back the next day. Always wanting to be the leader in any project, I raised my hand and promptly was appointed to see that the doll's wrap was laundered.

When I arrived home from school that day, I could tell right off that I had probably acted in haste. First off, the weather had turned bad. Then the kids were crying, my mother was busy and harried as usual. In short, I knew that I had taken on a hopeless task. I washed the wrap and hung it to dry, but with the weather damp and cold, there was no way to get it dry. True, there was a fire in the fireplace, but with the entire family hovered around it; there was no way to dry anything. Finally, I put the flat irons on the coals in the fireplace, hoping to iron it dry, but from being in the fireplace, the irons had ashes and soot clinging to them, and some of this came off onto the damp cloth as I ironed. By this time, it was getting late and I had other things to do, so I folded the wrap to take to school, and hoped for the best.

The next morning I handed it to the teacher, but nothing was said. Then later that morning, the mother of a classmate who lived only about a hundred yards from the school came to our schoolroom and I saw the teacher slip something to her. I doubt that anyone noticed it but me. That afternoon, the lady came to the school again, and I saw her slip something to the teacher. Then I knew what was going on. The teacher had gotten word to her somehow that she needed a favor, and the lady had done the favor, laundered and ironed the wrap, both evidently hoping that no one had noticed what they were doing.

The lady in this story had been a childhood friend of my mother, and was a staunch member of the church we attended. Regardless of what one might say about other members of the same church, here was one woman who in my opinion practiced her religion on a day to day basis. Anyone who will go to great lengths to save the feelings of a child is, in my opinion, one of God's own. She has been gone for many years now, and probably the teacher also, but when I think of them, it is with the kindest of thoughts. No one ever mentioned this incident to me, I never told anyone at home about it, and I doubt that anyone ever knew of it but the two of them and me, and I only knew of it because I was observant.

The people we knew during the Depression were very different from those we know today, in the twenty-first century. They were simple, not highly educated, mostly white, sometimes flawed, people of mostly Celtic stock. They came from people who had already endured much, settling a wild new part of the country, and then fighting the Civil War, in which they had no vested interest. They had owned no plantations, but had ended up fighting anyway. Then they had seen their beloved southland considered "a little less than" since the Civil War, which is always the loser's lot. Coming from a background such as this, can anyone wonder that these people might sometimes be considered a bit eccentric by today's standards? I think not. However, some of them were good and kindly eccentrics, as the preceding story indicates.

VI

Getting an Education, No Matter What

Both our father and our mother had a very high degree of native intelligence, but because of the circumstances in which they grew up, my mother was not highly educated, and my father not at all. They both regretted it all of their lives. Perhaps because of the paucity of opportunities in their own lives, they had very noble ambitions for their children, and considered education to be the doorway to opportunity. Thus education had first priority in our family. Before school began each year, my father would make sure he had enough money to buy all our books. On the day school opened, after we all got home, he would gather up all the book lists, drive the seven miles to town, and get them filled. None of us ever had to go to school a single day without our books, as many children did during that era. When this happened, they would have to sit double in the desk with another student and share a book.

When The Depression descended upon us, my sister and I were attending an elementary and junior high school built on the same spot where a one-room schoolhouse had stood, and where my mother during her entire seven years of schooling had been taught by a Miss Madge McDonald. Miss Madge, as she was respectfully called, had taught through the eighth grade there, but my mother had dropped out after the seventh grade, because she didn't have proper clothes, and, I suspect, because she was needed at home. After the death of her mother, her father had married again and now had a very large second family. The old school had been torn down some years before my time, and a larger, somewhat more up-to-date building erected. It was a large white two story affair with absolutely nothing to recommend it architecturally.

The lower floor was for classes. It consisted of one large room with folding doors that were used to divide it into two rooms for classes, or folded back when a larger room was needed for school activities and community doings. At first, all the grades were taught in these two rooms. Eventually, as the enrollment increased another, much smaller room was attached to the side of the building. The upper floor of the building was reserved for the Odd Fellows Lodge, which was very active in the community at that time. The Odd Fellows were a service organization somewhat like the Masons. A man's standing in the community was greatly enhanced by his membership in the organization. The second floor therefore was more or less sacred ground and the students were not allowed to tread there. They told us there was a Billy goat up there, and the door to the stairs was kept locked. In any event, i wouldn't have been safe, for the stairs were very high and very steep.

The rest rooms were two "two-holers" (one for boys and one for girls) which sat about a hundred yards behind the schoolhouse. There was no toilet tissue and no water. For drinking water, there was a well with a hand pump situated in the middle of the school yard, between the schoolhouse and the church which stood nearby. A few lucky students had metal folding cups, but most of us drank out of our hands or from a cup fashioned from scrap paper.

Eventually, another building was constructed nearby. This building just missed being modern. It appeared modern on the outside, but there still were no rest rooms, and only two classrooms. Sometime later there was another room built onto the rear, and the seventh, eight, and ninth grades were taught there.

The schoolrooms were heated by pot-bellied stoves, one in each room. The principal would build a fire in each stove before school opened each morning, and it would be up to the teacher to keep the fire going the rest of the day. If the coal scuttle became empty during the day, one of the boys would be sent to the coal bin behind the school to get more. A pan of water was usually kept simmering on the stove, to keep the air in the room from being too dry. On very cold mornings, after we had walked the long distance to school, over frozen ground, my feet and hands and face would have no feeling left in them. On such mornings, the teacher might let us stand near the stove until we got warm, and oh, how everything would hurt as the feeling began coming back. I remember once, the teacher was stirring the fire, and must have stirred it a bit too vigorously, and the stovepipe fell, scattering fire, stovepipe segments, soot and ashes all around the room. She sent for the principal, who came in quite a state of excitement. There was no fire department, or even fire extinguishers to call upon in those days. After enlisting the help of some of the larger boys, however, they got the fire extinguished and the mess cleaned up. Then someone helped him put the stovepipe back in place, and the school day continued.

When the Depression came, I was in the third grade in the large white building with the legendary Billy goat in the upper floor. I had heard one of the disgruntled teachers once call it "the chicken house", and in my private thoughts it has evermore been so. Two grades were always taught in one room by one teacher, and my class shared a room with the fourth grade. I really liked this, since I could be learning some of the next grade's lessons along with my own. One thing I remember learning from listening to the fourth grade lessons was how to recite in alphabetical order all the counties in the State of Alabama. Now, what use that has ever been to me is highly questionable, but that's how students were taught back then-- a great deal of memorizing of poems, lists, and so forth.

We had two play periods each day. The first one, about ten o'clock in the morning, was our recess, and the second was at noon, following lunch. There was no lunch room, and we ate our lunches at our desks. In the schoolyard afterward, we sometimes played a crude form of baseball, using a piece of barn board for a bat, and maybe a tennis ball that someone had brought to school. We also played Red Rover, Flying Dutchman, dodge ball, Farmer in the Dell, and one particularly creative game called Annie Over. To play Annie Over, we would choose sides, and each side would take up position on one side of the church building at the edge of the schoolyard. Then one side would throw a ball over the roof of the church, and the other side would catch it. Then there would be a wild chase around the church, with the person holding the ball trying to catch as many of the other side as possible. If one got caught, they had to join the opposing team, and the team with the most people won. I have often wondered how we played that game every day for many years and never broke a church window.

41

By the next year, when I was in the fourth grade, a new teacher had been sent to the school, and the classes were taught separately. In my school career, I had two really mean teachers, and she was one of them. Teachers back then got away with many aberrant practices, and much cruelty that wouldn't be tolerated today. Some of them may have been poorly trained. Almost without exception, they were "normal school" graduates. A normal school was a college that trained only teachers, and the course was only two years in duration. In addition, during the Depression, the teachers in that area were paid very poorly. The one instance that I knew of, the teacher was only paid about Forty dollars a month, so there may not have been the incentive for excellence that there might have been. As I look back on it now, I think this particular teacher may have been emotionally unstable, her meanness was so extreme. She was constantly beating someone. One day I saw her beat a boy over the shoulders with a yardstick until it splintered and broke. Every day we had to line up outside to come in from recess. One cold day someone talked in line or we didn't line up straight, some small thing, and she made us all stand outside in the cold for a long while. Another time, someone told her that I had been whispering in class and she made me and some others stay after school (she went home and left us alone in the schoolroom) to write a certain sentence 500 times. It was a terrible waste of paper and pencil when such things were hard to come by, and when I was finished it was almost dark. By the time I walked the long distance home alone, it was first dark when I arrived. The road home was very lonely, there being only woods once one left the vicinity of the school.

Once, when I was in about the third grade, I became ill at school, and the teacher told me I could go home. Going home meant walking the mile and a half home by myself on a very lonely road. As it happened, the rural mail carrier came by on his route, and gave me a ride home. This was strictly against the law, I am sure, but he probably felt sorry for me.

The years slipped by, the Depression seemed endless, and our family struggled on. It was never easy, but by the time I reached the seventh grade, all the grades above the sixth had been moved to the consolidated school about six miles away, and the school bus route had been extended to our homestead and beyond. This included not only us, but also the students who had formerly had to walk much greater distances than we did. This helped immeasurably. For one thing, it put an end to the harassment my sister and I had suffered at the hands of certain students who came from further up the road. All those years, we had suffered every kind of harassment as we walked to school, and we had no choice but to suffer in silence, since we were outnumbered and some of our torturers could be really vicious. Many things happened that we never told our father, fearing what he might have done. Once, when I had to walk to school by myself because my sister was out sick, the harassment reached a new level and I was very afraid. After a few days of this, my mother came and hid on the side of the road to see for herself what was happening. The next day she sent a note to school and got it stopped for a time.

When I was in the sixth grade, my teacher was a man who was also principal of the school. He was a good teacher, I thought, and I really liked him. I thought he also liked me, because I was a good student and didn't cause any trouble. Then one day something happened that I thought was very cruel. We had had an assignment to write a story about something, actually anything we chose to. Everyone else in the class wrote about some small incident that had happened in their lives. I, however, tried writing fiction for the first time in my life. At this point in time, I don't remember exactly what it was about, but I do remember that I was very proud of it. When the time came to hand out the papers and discuss the stories, the teacher said to the class "I want to read something to you", and proceeded to read my paper. The class howled with laughter, and he laughed along with them, while I sat there fighting tears. It finally was over, and he didn't tell the class whose paper it was, and I never confronted him about it. It taught me a lesson, however, as all injustices do. It also made me stronger, as all injustices do, once they are overcome. I was told that after I went on to another school and was promoted twice in one year, he bragged on me, but his opinion meant little to me at that point.

My first year at the new school, I made two grades, as already mentioned, so the next year I was in high school. This was because

I had attained a certain level on an IQ test. High school was an especially painful time for me. Having skipped a grade, I was one of the younger ones in the class, and considerably less sophisticated than some of the others. The most painful difference, however, was the socioeconomic gap. Most of my classmates had parents who worked for the Tennessee Company, and drew a paycheck each week, while my father's income was sporadic. In any given week, he might have a good week and do well financially, or he might not make a dime. The money from the good times had to be saved for the bad times. On the other hand, even in the depth of the Depression, the people who worked for the Tennessee Company had a steady income, however small it might be. Moreover, many of them lived in company houses, some of which were very, very nice, and paid very little rent. This meant that those students had money for clothes, which we didn't have. They also lived near, or in, town, and had access to things we never got to even see. Some of the boys drove school buses. That job paid fifteen dollars per month, but at that time, fifteen dollars a month was a fortune. The whole situation made me feel "less than", and my family pride being what it is, it made me very sad. I felt that the fact that I worked hard was unappreciated, and that the whole high school situation was just one more thing to be gotten through. The teachers also seemed to favor the students who had more money and more economic advantages. One teacher in particular was especially mean to some of us, while at the same time inflating the grades of the football players. High school as a whole was traumatic for me, and on receiving my diploma, I felt only relief that it was over. We did not have a senior prom, but did have a senior "banquet", held in the lunch room of the school, and I don't imagine the food was all that elegant. I didn't attend, because I had nothing to wear. The football team also had a "football banquet", for which the food was mostly donated.

We had no entertainment. Movies were a quarter at that time, a hamburger cost a nickel, a coke another nickel, and an ice cream cone the same. However, with no money these were only things I heard of, not things I had any part in. My chances to go to town were extremely rare. Sometimes, but not very often, some of the neighbors would come in and we would roast peanuts or make molasses taffy. This was always a treat for them, some of whom were genuinely poor. I remember once when my sister had spent a good part of a Saturday making crème-filled cookies for the next week's lunches. That night some neighbor kids came in and she offered them some of the cookies. I suppose they were really hungry for sweets, for they kept going back to the cookie bin, uninvited, until not one cookie was left. There were many reasons why we didn't always have a school lunch, but my sister never stopped trying. Many of her efforts were nullified by such incidents.

About the school buses, mentioned above. They were big, rattling affairs, with one long bench type seat down each side, and two more in the middle. There were no forward-facing seats, and certainly no seat belts. I'm sure they had no "all-weather" tires, either. When it would rain and the red clay in the chirt road made the going very slippery the buses sometimes couldn't make it. My sister remembers bus number 59 having to be pushed up Bell Hill, a long, fairly steep hill near the school, by some of the students. The bus would stop at the bottom of the hill, everyone would get out, and some of the larger boys would start pushing. At the top of the hill, everyone would get back on the bus.

There was one bright spot in my senior year of high school. All through my childhood and through the soul-destroying indignities of the Great Depression, my one dream had been to somehow, someday go to college. Attending college was my idea of how to get out of the environment in which I had grown up, away from the lack of opportunities, the lack of culture, the ignorance and poverty which surrounded us. There seemed little hope of ever attaining my dream, but it was the only dream I had. I never dreamed of marriage and a family as most girls in that day and age did. I just wanted to get out of there and get as far away as I could.

The pastor of our small country church was a ministerial student at Birmingham-Southern College. Our church didn't have a parsonage, so to avoid the pastor having to drive the twenty miles back to Birmingham in between the morning and evening services, the ladies of the church would take turns inviting the preacher to

Sunday dinner. The preachers and others in the church always enjoyed coming to our house, since we always had plenty of good farm-fresh food and my mother was an excellent cook. One Sunday when he had dinner at our house, he questioned me about school and what my aims were after graduation. I told him I would like to go to college, but there seemed little hope of it. Then, just out of the blue, he said that he would try to get a scholarship for me to a school he had attended in Tennessee. The very next week he made a trip to Tennessee and did what he could. He wasn't able to get a scholarship, but he did get financial help in the form of a loan. My parents were to pay thirty dollars a month and the balance would be paid by the loan, which I was to repay in four years, when it was assumed I would be graduated. That young pastor died many years ago, at much too young an age. With every thought of him, I thank God that his life touched mine just when I needed someone. I found out later that his choice of schools wasn't necessarily the best for me, but at least I was in college, and away from where I had grown up.

The following September I went away to college, one of only three in my graduating class of thirty six who did so. I remember I worked in the fields up until two weeks before I was to leave. Then I had that two weeks to make all of my school clothes. I had ordered dress material from the Sears catalog. The information from the college had said that evening clothes were mandatory, so the first thing I tackled was an evening dress. Never having been to a formal affair, or even seen an evening dress except in pictures, I did the best I could. Not being able to afford but one evening dress, I had ordered blue satin, not realizing that September in Tennessee is much too warm for satin. It was an off-the-shoulder affair with straps and a jacket to match. I finished the rest of my wardrobe, the skirts, blouses and a pair of pajamas (these from feed sacks), packed everything in an old trunk and an old suitcase that my father had had when he was a young man, and was off on my very first train ride. Up until then I had never been more than thirty miles from home.

Arriving in Tennessee, I was met at the station by a representative of the school and taken to the campus. There I was assigned to a room and told when mealtime was. The meals were served family style, eight people to a table, and we sang songs and choruses before sitting down, much like summer camp today. The meals were very well planned, and the food good.

About a week or two after school opened, we had to attend our first formal affair of the year. It was a mandatory thing. Most of the girls got dressed in frilly white or pastel summer evening dresses, but I for lack of alternatives put on my blue satin train wreck of a dress, product of my home sewing. I did not enjoy the formal affairs, always feeling somewhat like I imagine a June bug might feel in a butterfly garden. Another disaster was my housecoat. I had never even seen or heard of such a thing as a housecoat until then. Had I known I could have sewn one from feed sacks. At this school, a housecoat was mandatory, since male students lived in the same dormitory, on a different floor, but sometimes came on our floor. Heaven forbid that you should allow a male student to see you in your pajamas.

Anyway, I wrote and told my mother that I needed a housecoat. My mother, who never ever went to town, probably didn't know what that was, either. Just as in pioneer days, my father took care of everything in town and my mother stayed home, took care of the place, and told him of anything that was needed from town. In the twentieth century, this plan did not work well, especially with my uneducated father. My mother told him that I needed a housecoat, so he went to town and to Erlick's, his favorite store, and told the lady there he wanted a housecoat for his daughter who was away in college. She asked him what size and he didn't have a clue. Then, I suppose she asked how old I was and he said seventeen, so she ordered a housecoat in size eighteen. At the time I was maybe a size eight. It took weeks and weeks for the housecoat to come, and for my mother to send it on to me. In the meantime, I had to stay in my room at night. With the boys living in the same dorm, although on a different floor, and sometimes coming onto our floor if they had reason to do so, I had to stay out of sight. Since our bathroom was some distance down the hall from my room, this was downright inconvenient---not the bathroom part--I was just glad not to still be traipsing to a privy. It was just that I hated staying in my room to avoid running into a male student who might be in the hall.

Then one night, the most embarrassing thing of all happened. We had a fire drill. When the fire alarm rang, everyone was supposed to go to the lobby of the building. I put that off as long as I dared, but when there was no one on the floor but me, I became concerned that the place might really be on fire. Timidly, I went down the hall and descended the long circular staircase into the lobby wearing my feed sack pajamas. Everyone laughed good naturedly, but I was majorly embarrassed.

Finally one day a package came, and it was the housecoat. It wasn't actually a housecoat, but more of a housedress, with a zipper up the front, not what I had envisioned at all. I had to take my showers in a communal shower with several other girls and anything as cumbersome to get out of and into as that was really inconvenient, and it was miles too big. However, I at least had something to wear over my pajamas, and I never let my parents know of my disappointment. As for the evening dress, I managed later in the year to get another, fancier one and my mother crocheted a pair of white evening gloves for me to wear with it. I still have the gloves.

If the reader has been wondering through all of this, why I didn't just go out and buy a housecoat, there were two reasons. First, I had no money, Secondly, even if I had had money, I wouldn't have been allowed to leave the campus and walk uptown without a teacher escort. We couldn't just run out and buy things.

Another thing I was lacking most of the year was a Bible. This was a religious school, and students used their Bibles constantly. Any lack of a Bible was severely looked down upon. Finally, out of the few coins my mother managed to send me from the sale of eggs and milk to the neighbors, I managed to save a dollar and a half, a nickel here, a dime there. I then sent off to Sears for a Bible I had seen in their catalog, with the words of Jesus in red. I was so proud of it when it came. When I went home at the end of the school year, my mother was fascinated with my nice Bible, and promptly took it for her own use. She had never in her life owned a Bible except a very small thing, about three and a half inches by five inches, with print so small I'm sure she wouldn't have been able to read it at that time.

She had paid ten cents for it soon after she and my father were married. My beautiful Bible with print large enough that she could read it and with the words of Jesus in red was a feast for her eyes and a blessing to her life. She used it until it was battered and worn; then, just before she died, she had it rebound, with my name in gold letters on the cover, just like before, and returned it to me. It is one of my greatest treasures.

Time Staggered on. I didn't enjoy certain aspects of the college curriculum. For one thing, the entire atmosphere was too religion-saturated. I consider myself a very spiritual person, but religion non stop all day long is not something I could feel comfortable with, when I had gone there in hopes of getting trained to earn a living. I did well in my English courses, and for the first time in my school career, I began to enjoy history. For a session or two, the English professor called on me to teach. I still remember the subjects we were studying at the time--the writers, Addison and Steele, and the newspapers, *Spectator* and *Tatler*.

Of course, there still were many embarrassments because I didn't have proper clothes. The girls had to always wear dresses and stockings. The rayon hose we wore at the time were not expensive by today's standards, but when you have no money, a pair of stockings is out of reach. I would wear my one pair of stockings (which was as much as I ever had) until the feet wore out, and then turn the feet down so the holes wouldn't show. The legs would then be baggy and ugly, and sometimes still there would be no money and no stockings coming from home. I thought the school rules were very silly and very unfair to students in my circumstance. Many of the girls who were on scholarships or work-study programs had well-to-do relatives who could send them a dress now and then, or certainly a pair of stockings. Hats were another sore point with me. The girls had to wear hats to church, and church was mandatory. I did well to afford one hat, let alone several, and it was embarrassing to wear the same hat to church each Sunday.

To make a bad matter worse, I had been assigned to a room with a girl who had the reputation of being extremely hard to get along with. I found that her reputation was well earned. Being an only child of a well-to-do Georgia widow, she was enormously spoiled and self-centered. Her mother owned the only dry goods store in a small Georgia town, and could easily furnish her daughter with the clothes and other things needed for dormitory living. She seemed to have no understanding of what it meant to come from a large family, or to be without money. At the time, we could do a load of laundry in the machine on the top floor for a quarter and hang it to dry on the clotheslines there. Most of the time, I didn't have a quarter, and when I did, I had to wash the things I wore from day to day. I admit that as a result, my bedspread did get to be a bit grubby, and one day when she was throwing one of her famous fits, she really let me have it about my bedspread. There was nothing I could do but take it and say nothing. After all, we were supposed to be in a religious school. Some religion, I thought.

Another time that I really wanted to wring her neck was concerned with religion. Every night at lights out time, before going to bed, all the women in our dormitory would gather at a certain place in the dormitory and hold a prayer meeting. I saw nothing wrong with that. One night however, it became charismatic, with shouting, talking in tongues, and generally carrying on. The next day it was the talk of the school, how the spirit had moved among the group, producing a mini revival. I made the mistake of saying that I hadn't felt anything, to which my roommate responded "well, if you didn't feel anything last night, there is something seriously wrong with you". Again, I took it and said nothing, remembering that I was on the more or less hallowed ground of a religious school.

Everyone in this school, both men and women were allowed membership in one of a number of fraternities and sororities. They weren't like the sororities and fraternities one usually finds on college campuses. They belonged to no national organization, charged no dues, and were strictly social clubs, with no promise of future social or professional benefits or prestige. At the end of the year, each sorority and fraternity had some kind of a celebration to end the year on a pleasant note. My sorority planned an evening in Chattanooga with dinner at one of the nice hotels there. The charge was three dollars and fifty cents per member, and of course, as usual, I had not a cent. One of the girls in the sorority offered to lend me the money, but I wouldn't accept the loan, knowing that I would have no way to repay it. I stood under the portico at the front entrance and watched the bus pull away with every member of the sorority but me. When you're seventeen years old and never been anywhere, such an experience can hurt, and it did.

When I returned home at the end of the school year, my mother informed me that my father did not intend to pay the thirty dollars a month for me to attend school in Tennessee any more. I pretended to be disappointed, but inside, I was doing a buck dance. My father had never liked having to make payments on anything. The monthly payments came around much too regular for him. On learning that, I went to Birmingham-Southern College, a small Methodist-sponsored school, about twenty miles from my home and registered. They seemed more than happy to put me on the National Youth Administration Program, sponsored by Eleanor Roosevelt, whereby I could borrow part of my tuition and work in the school library to earn the rest. The job paid twenty cents an hour. I still needed a Bible, so to replace the lost one I went to Woolworth's and bought one for fifty cents. It wasn't a very good one, and barely lasted until I graduated.

For the next two years, I lived with my sister and her husband in a three-room shotgun in town, sleeping on an army cot in the kitchen. Every morning I would walk six blocks to the streetcar line, ride for an hour and a half, then walk eight more blocks uphill to the college. I took a full load of courses, and with working in the library, I rarely arrived back at the shotgun before dark. I never had any lunch, but my sister would usually have a pot of vegetable soup or something similar when I arrived home. She had transformed the back yard into a vegetable garden, and we ate a lot of vegetables. She tells the story now that once while eating dinner I remarked that we had tomatoes prepared three different ways. (Was I ever really that rude?)

Clothes were a problem still, but nothing like what they had been at the former school. Everyone wore saddle shoes and ankle socks, sweaters and skirts. In the winter many of the girls wore their mothers' fur coats with their bare legs and saddle shoes. Most of the "townies" belonged to sororities and fraternities. Many of the girls flaunted the fact that they had been "pinned" by their boyfriends. That is, they had been given their boyfriend's fraternity pin to wear with their expensive sweaters and pearls. Being "pinned" was tantamount to being engaged. Working in the library, I would hear them talking about their "bids" to this or that fraternity party. It was all very foreign to me, and I wondered how the sorority and fraternity process worked, how a certain person happened to be chosen for membership, while others were passed over. I was invited to join several academic societies, but that was not the same.

My father paid the three dollars per week that my streetcar tickets cost. He also paid for my first set of books. After that, as one semester ended and another began, I traded in the books I had just finished with, and used the trade-in value to buy the new books I needed. During Christmas vacation my senior year I was lucky enough to land a job in the S.H. Kress five and dime store. I worked in the candy department for a dollar and a half per day. Of that amount, I netted a dollar and forty six cents a day, after their having taken out four cents for social security tax. It helped a great deal when school reopened after the holidays. I remember at quitting time on Christmas Eve, the manager of the store came to the candy counter and told us we could have whatever we wanted for free. I selected several bags of Christmas candy to take home to my younger brothers and sisters, knowing that they probably wouldn't be getting many Christmas goodies otherwise.

I wore my feed sack dresses, and my thrift store shoes and men's socks that my father had picked up in town, and tried not to mind that I had come from a different world from the one in which I was trying to survive. I would use the three hours per day that I was on the streetcar to study. On weekends I went home to the country, and usually cleaned my mother's house. She still had five children at home at that time, and my sister and I were not there to help, as we had been in former years.

I graduated cum laude in 1940, having finished college in three years instead of the usual four. My parents were the only relatives who attended the graduation. During the proceedings, my father overheard someone saying that a degree from that school wasn't worth much, that one needed an advance degree to go along with it. It really upset him. My father didn't understand the difference between a liberal arts education and a university-attained vocation-specific education. Actually, Birmingham-Southern is one of the best liberal arts colleges in the country, and I have always felt that as difficult as those years were, I got a very good education there. They told us they were training us for life, not just for earning a living, and I think they did that.

As I graduated from college, the Great Depression was finally coming to an end. The country didn't really pull out of it until two years later, when the nation began arming for the military battles ahead. Thus began another very difficult four years, with two of my brothers away in the service of their country. However, once that was over, and in the years since that time, my family has gone on to good fortune far beyond our childhood dreams. I really believe that the generation that grew up during the Great Depression, went on to save the world for democracy in World War II and then built an economy that is the envy of the world. It is, in the view of many, the greatest generation our country has ever produced. No matter how bad we think things are, some unexpected good nearly always results, and this is the good that came from the Great Depression. Echoes of the great generation still continue. Some of the sons of Depression era kids are now at the helm of our government. Their grandsons are fighting for freedom in Afghanistan, and around the world. The good and the greatness forged in the fires of the Great Depression continue.

VII

Chop the Wood, Hoe the Peas, Bring the Water, Mind the Baby

I remember the Depression not as a time of hunger, as many people of my generation do. We never went hungry. What I remember is the back breaking, never ending work beginning when I was just nine years old. I can't blame my parents for any of it, for they worked incredibly hard also. My mother was keeping the farm and family functioning while my father was off with the cattle truck, either buying and selling, or rounding up strays. Everyone in the family had to work except the very youngest. I hated every minute of it, and I hated the fact that my father was a farmer. Why couldn't he work in one of the steel mills like the other kids' fathers, I wondered. I also hated the fact that we lived isolated on the farm, with no playtime or anyone with whom to play except my younger brothers, whom I was always babysitting when I wasn't working. I spent my childhood dreaming of going away to college someday. My dreams never went beyond college. I didn't know enough about what careers there were to think along those lines.

From age nine, when the Depression hit, until I left home, my summers were spent in the fields, planting, hoeing, and gathering. During spring planting time, my sister and I would remove our school clothes when we arrived home from school, put on something old, and hit the fields, planting corn or peas, setting out sweet potato slips, or spreading fertilizer. When school was out for the summer and the summer sun beat down mercilessly, we would be in the field all day, hoeing corn or peas, or putting stakes to the pole beans. When we weren't working in the fields, there was the laundry, ironing, scrubbing floors and cleaning house to be done. Then there was the fruit and vegetables to be gathered and canned. My mother had planted approximately a hundred fruit trees of various kinds on the terraces of the ten acres above our house, where usually peas or corn were grown. When the Depression came, they were just beginning to bear their best harvests. I didn't mind gathering the fruit. In June, I would gather basket after basket of peaches, which we would then can. Sitting in a circle in the screened-in back porch, with a huge washtub full of peaches between us, we would peel and slice. Every so often my mother would go and remove the pressure cooker full of jars from the stove, fill more jars, then fill the pressure cooker again. Later in the year we would go through the same process with the apples, pears, and plums.

The vegetable canning went on all summer. We canned peas, butterbeans, corn, tomatoes, soup mix, chow-chow, and made all kinds of jellies and jams. My mother also made kraut, packing it in a large crockery churn, and hominy. I always liked hominy, especially the kind she made, with the germs of the corn kernels left on. In our spare time we would pick wild blackberries or huckleberries for the making of jams and jellies, and we had several fig trees from which we gathered purple figs and made preserves. All in all, we would can enough fruits and vegetables to last our large family until the next canning season. Most of the jars were half gallons, everything except the jams and jellies, and they went into quarts. The kraut and hominy were not canned. The kraut was packed in salt, and only taken out of the crock as needed. The hominy was made in small batches, and used while fresh.

Besides providing food for ourselves, we also raised vegetables for the market. We never sold corn, because that was needed for cornmeal for ourselves and food for the cattle. My father would take truckloads of un-shucked corn to a place called the hammermill and have it pulverized, the grain, shucks, cobs, the whole works, for feed for the cows and horse. When we ran out of cornmeal, we would shuck and shell a large cotton sack full of corn for him to take to the gristmill. Bread made from it tasted better than that made from any corn meal in the markets today. We stored our corn harvest in a rat-proof corncrib of my father's design. My uncle, who was staying with us at the time, built the crib, which was about fifteen by twenty feet. It stood on tall heart pine supporting logs, and over the top of each supporting log we placed upside down a fifty-pound lard can. No rat or squirrel could possibly get beyond such a barrier, and we enjoyed the benefits of a pest proof crib from then on.

Peas were one crop that always sold well in the markets in the summertime. Housewives, when they could afford it, would buy them by the bushel, and can them for the wintertime just as we did. Consequently, my parents always wanted several acres planted in peas. I can remember my sister and I hoeing peas over the entire ten acres above the barn at the top of the hill. It was the first ten acres our parents had bought when they were newlyweds. In the fall, the same long pea rows we had hoed during the summer had to be picked. We also planted about fifteen acres in corn, a watermelon patch, a peanut patch, and always a large vegetable garden. One year we planted a large field of sorghum. The man who lived on our p lace in the next county owned a sorghum mill and would work "on the shares". This meant that he would take, as his pay, part of the sorghum syrup that was produced from the cane. The man came with his mill and they hitched our horse Nell to the contraption, and had her walk around in a circle all day long, turning the mill. I remember the juice pouring out of the cane and into the cooking pan, and then being skimmed as it cooked, to remove any impurities. What was left after the cane was crushed in the mill was called pumice. Our Uncle Sam, who was in charge of Nell, let her eat too much of the pumice, which resulted in a bad case of horse colic, and she died that night. This was a sad time for our entire family, since we had all grown up with Nell, and she had been a very hard working and gentle horse, loved by all the family.

When we came home from school each school day afternoon the first thing we would do, of course, was change our clothes. Then we would grab a snack. This usually was a baked sweet potato, a pocket full of peanuts, or a cold biscuit or slic e of cornbread with butter and sugar or sorghum syrup inside. Then we would hit the pea patch and pick peas until almost dark and time to do the evening chores. Then with our father supervising, we would take the peas to the barn at the top of the hill where there was an expanse of smooth Bermuda grass. There we would spread the peas on the Bermuda grass to be freshened by the cool night air and the dew. The next morning our father would have us up early, helping him sack the peas into burlap bags and ready for market before we ate breakfast.

Then, after having eaten his own breakfast, he would be off to town to make deliveries to the various grocery stores.

Another early morning chore for my sister and me was to help our father dress out a beef. He always did the butchering in the late afternoon and let the carcass cool in the night air before skinning it out. We always helped him do both. In my earliest memories, he would kill a beef by first hitting it on the head with a sledge hammer and then cutting its throat. Later on he began using a twenty-two rifle. Then he would gut the animal and heist it by a windlass to "cure" in the night air. This was long before there was any electricity or refrigeration in our area. The tripe was saved and cleaned to be sold in town, and the entrails were usually buried. The heart was saved, and either sold or eaten by the family.

The next morning very early our father would awaken us to help him skin out and saw down the beef. He never trusted us with the skinning knives, probably afraid that we would knick the beef and make it less saleable, or worse still, hurt ourselves. Our job was mostly to hold the beef steady while he did the skinning, and again while he sawed down and quartered it. With an ordinary carpenter's saw, he would start at the tail and saw straight down the center of the backbone to the neck. Then again we would have to hold it steady while he cut the carcass into quarters. Then it would be wrapped in white cloth, usually a sheet made from feed sacks, and loaded into the truck. Then we could go in to breakfast. For an animal lover like me, there was a lot of heartbreak connected to the butchering, but it was the life that was ours, so we persevered, and tried to help the family survive.

In the late summer, we would sometimes pull fodder. Fodder is the green fronds of the corn plants. If it is stripped from the stalks while still green and dried, it makes very good winter food for the cattle. We would strip the stalk until we had a good handful of fronds, and then pull another frond with which to tie the bunch to the stalk to dry. Without a doubt, this was the most disagreeable work I have ever done, because of the "saddlebacks". Saddlebacks are a small insect, a bit larger than a fly, with a furry appearance, a design resembling a saddle on its back, and the worst sting I have ever had the misfortune to experience. It will make you want to die.

Another thing we had to do was to dig the sweet potatoes. First, we would go through the patch and remove all the vines. Hogs love sweet potato vines, so we would put them in the hog pen. Then the plowman, whoever it happened to be, would go down the hilled rows with a huge turning plow, and unearth the potatoes. We would follow after with produce hampers and gather the potatoes. Then we would turn the hogs into the potato patch to root out and devour what we had missed.

After the potatoes were harvested, they had to be hilled out for the winter. To do this, we would dig a long, shallow hole in the ground, and line it with pine straw. On top of this we would place the potatoes, cover them with more pine straw, and then a tarp. On top of all of this, we would pile earth, ending with something resembling a little hillock. This would keep the sweet potatoes fresh all winter, and they could easily be retrieved for cooking by digging into the edge of the potato hill.

Another fall chore was harvesting the peanuts. Here again, they would first have to be unearthed by a turning plow. Then we would go along the rows, pulling the plants from the dirt, shaking the dirt from each plant, and placing then so the peanuts would get the full force of the sun to dry. They would be left that way for a day or two and when sufficiently dry, we would have to separate the peanuts from the plants, put then into burlap bags and store them in the corn crib. Then the corn would have to be harvested and put into the corncrib. This was a lot of hard work, but I remember what a good feeling it was, seeing huge amounts of corn going into the crib, and knowing that it represented our independence. There is no other feeling quite like independence, even to a child.

When the corn was harvested, the dry peas had to be picked. There would be many bushels of them, and we would thresh them on the barn floor or the crib floor, wherever there was room. They then would be placed in weevil-proof containers, for winter eating and for next year's seeds.

In the afternoon when the fieldwork was done, there were always chores to do. The first thing was to go into the woods, find the milk cows and drive them home. Our mother usually accompanied us. After the cows were in the barn, she would feed and milk them, take the milk to the house, some hundred yards away, run it through a strainer, and put it in a cool place. My jobs always were feeding the chickens, gathering the eggs, sometimes feeding the hogs and bringing water from the spring a quarter of a mile away. In addition, I always was the dishwasher. I really hated this on cold winter nights when the rest of the family had settled down by the one fireplace we kept going, the kitchen was frigid, and there was little if any hot water. With our large family and the one or two "extras" we always seemed to have staying with us, I was washing dishes for near a dozen people. I didn't mind the dishwashing itself; in fact I rather liked washing dishes in warmer weather. It was just the circumstances, and the fact that I was just a child.

I always liked feeding the chickens. We always had a large flock, and when I called them in the afternoon, they would all come scurrying to get the grain I tossed about the back yard for them. Then I would go into the chicken house to gather the eggs. Sometimes a hen would still be on the nest, and when I ran my hand under a hen to retrieve the eggs, she would cackle, flap her wings, and scatter dust and mites. As a result of breathing this, I had childhood histoplasmosis, a condition that has continued for a lifetime.

Our hogs were usually fed kitchen slop, corn and shorts. As I remember, shorts are a by-product from the making of products such as oleomargarine and cooking oil from cottonseed. Other than being fed twice a day, the hogs didn't require much care except when the weather turned cold. Then it was my job to take an old bed sheet, go into the woods, and rake huge piles of pine straw, put them on the sheet, gather up the corners, and carry it to the hog pen for a bed for the hogs. This usually required several trips. I didn't mind this job, because I loved going into the woods, especially the spot where the huge longleaf pines stood in a thick carpet of pine needles.

59

To keep the fireplace going in the wintertime, and the cook stove supplied with fuel all year long, our father would fell a huge oak tree. Then, all the family that were old enough to work would help with the sawing and chopping required to convert it into stove wood and fireplace logs. One of our evening chores was to bring in enough wood for the evening and the next morning for the fireplace and the cook stove. This job usually fell to whichever one of us our mother could catch who wasn't busy with other chores.

To start the fires, kindling was needed, and what we used for kindling was the heart pine knots that remained from the felling of the virgin timber that had blanketed the area twenty years before. As the trees were felled they were stripped of their branches, which were left on the ground to rot. With the passage of years, all that was left was the knots, where one branch joined another. These were heart pine, and probably would never have rotted, had they been left there. It always fell to my sister and me to go into the woods and gather pine knots for kindling with which to build fires. We would make trip after trip into the woods, perhaps a half-mile, to gather as many knots as we could carry in our arms, bring them to the fence row of the upper field and throw them over into the field. When we had gathered a big enough pile, we would climb the fence and armload by armload carry them to the house through the ten acre field. I remember once when some really bad weather was coming, and there was nothing with which to start a fire, we had to go on a gathering foray. As my sister and I went into the woods, it began to snow, but we scoured the cold woods for knots, carried load after load to the fence and then repeated the routine on the other side of the fence, as the snow came down harder and harder. Finally we got it all to the house. I don't remember how many inches of snow we got that time, (we never got any really big snows in the southland) but however many, we had fires by which to warm ourselves and cook our food.

As one can see, I didn't have any idle time as a child. What might otherwise have been idle time was occupied with baby-sitting. I was always considered a less productive worker than my sister, who was six years older, so I was always given the job of taking care of the younger children. There were five younger than me, and I usually had two or three to take care of. Day after day, when the weather was warm, I would take them into the woods and gather flowers, which we would take home to our mother. I never let one of them get snake bitten, fall into the creek, fall off a bluff, or get hurt in any way. But I left my childhood in those woods; a lonely, lost childhood spent taking care of children when I should have been developing social skills, interacting with people my own age. If a childhood is lost, it is gone forever, and can never be retrieved. I don't blame anyone. My mother had more work to do than any two other women could have done, my father did the best he could with his limited education, and my sister worked hard. It was just the terrible times we were born into, a vexing, trying interlude between two world wars.

VIII

Yes, You Have To Go To Church

Nowadays, when people are unhappy, they tend to blame the government. They march, they riot, they burn their neighborhoods, and sometimes shoot their co-workers. It was not that way in the 1930's. At that time, people were more malleable and compliant, even humble. They were hungry, yes, but there were no food riots. For the most part, they made do with what they had, or could get as handouts from the government, dug ditches, took in laundry, fed their families on gravy and biscuits, and sometimes went without food so their children could eat. Our country is so different today, I shudder to think what might ensue if our economy should again become seriously depressed.

In the early twentieth century, most Americans, and especially those in the south, depended heavily on their religious faith to see them through hard times and eventually reward them with good times, even if the latter only came when heaven was attained. So it happened that in the throes of the Great Depression, many people in the area where we lived, turned not to crime, rioting and mayhem, but to conservative religion, figuring, I suppose, that we had somehow brought the Depression on ourselves by our lack of piety. Several new, very conservative Protestant sects came into being, the old line Protestants became less progressive, more dogmatic, and more unforgiving of human shortcomings. Most radical of all were some of the radio preachers who began broadcasting about this time. They drew large numbers of listeners who never missed a broadcast, and since these same listeners made up part of the local congregations, the influence of the radio preachers crept into some of the churches.

I can't say that I ever enjoyed going to church. The preachers scared me half to death, preaching about the fires of hell and the unpardonable sin. They never explained on my level of understanding, just what constituted the unpardonable sin, so I would lie awake and wonder if I was beyond the reach of God, from having committed the unpardonable sin. My parents were of the old school who believed that if a preacher said something, one had better listen and heed, if one wanted to escape eternal damnation. Not until I went away to college and associated with preachers in a school setting did I learn that they are flawed human beings, just like everyone else, and that their interpretation of the gospel is sometimes also flawed.

Every Sunday morning when I was a child, I would say to my mother that I didn't want to go to church, and her answer was always the same, "yes, you have to go to church". So I would get ready and go. Always riding standing in the back of the cattle truck, which was the only vehicle the family had. The younger children rode in the cab with my older sister and my father. My mother never went to church at that time, since she was usually either pregnant, or recovering from the birth of a child.

One thing that I found particularly hurtful during this period was that I had to look after my oldest brother, four years younger than me, when we went to church. The youngest children were put into what was called the card class. In this class, each child was given a small card with a Biblical picture on one side and the corresponding Bible story on the other. The teacher, a dear elderly lady, would read the Bible story to the class, ask a few simple questions appropriate to their level of understanding, and then pass out home made sugar cookies to everyone. By the time my brother began going to Sunday school, it was long since time for me to move up to the next class, but my mother made me stay in the card class to look after him. It was so embarrassing, when all my peers had long ago moved up to the next level. I had to stay in that class with the "babies", and with him until he was almost old enough to start school, at which time I would have been ten years old, and all my peers had gone on and learned so much that I had missed out on. Rightly or wrongly, I really resented this, reasoning that it was uncalled for, and because I thought that if it was necessary, someone else could have taken over the job part of the time.

The preachers would preach against such things as the young people playing a backyard baseball game on Sunday afternoon (that was profaning the Lord's Day), dancing, or playing any kind of card games. Today that same church sponsors card games one morning a week. The fellowship in the church we attended was not always loving. I always felt that we were looked down upon because we were farmers, and had to work hard, and were always sunburned, when the ideal at that time was to be lily white. We also had to travel in a cattle truck, when the other families had cars. We never had any leisure time when all the other families had fathers who worked at public works, and their families had many hours of leisure, in which to visit with their friends, play games, and develop social skills. Several times I heard girls in my Sunday school class make insulting remarks about me, my clothes, and my appearance, and didn't seem to care if I heard. I really disliked going to church. The church, we were told, was the place where God lived, and the Bible indicates that God is love. Putting those two thoughts together, one would expect the church to be a place where love lived, but as a child, I didn't find it so.

Most of the churches in our area held revival services each year during the summer months, to build up their membership. They usually would hire a hell fire and brimstone preacher to come and rain guilt down on the congregation. (Why couldn't he just have told those poor hungry people that God loved them, and understood what they were going through?) There was no air conditioning then, so sometimes the country churches would build brush arbors in which to hold their services. I remember attending services in a few of these. The flying bugs could be very annoying.

Some of the really super conservative denominations of Christendom that we had never heard of before became active in our area during this time. Their services were so different from anything we had ever experienced; we sometimes attended their revival services just to observe. Some or their practices, such as talking in tongues, as some enthusiastic members did, was new to us. Shouting, which had once been an honored tradition in the church that we attended, had largely died out by this time.

The most destructive part of the conservative movement which engulfed us during the Depression years, from my point of view, was that people became very critical, very unforgiving, of each other. The slightest transgression brought righteous criticism, often backed by a quotation from some minor Old Testament prophet. Young people were a favorite target, and especially young women. Luckily, no one in our family became a target of the gossips (that we knew of), since all we did was stay home and work. However, much harm was done, friendships were ruined, and reputations destroyed by this hyper-critical, unforgiving attitude, which was rampant in that area at that point in time.

IX

Keep Your Dress Down, Say "Yes, Sir" and "No, Sir"

When I was growing up during the Depression we were not taught to be afraid of strangers. There was no need of it. We knew everyone who lived in the area, and the only strangers were the harmless hungry people who passed by on the road or the railroad. We were taught that when someone knocked on the door and we answered, we were to greet whomever was there with a "good morning", or "good afternoon", not a curt "yes?" or just a questioning look, as one is likely to encounter today. We were to always answer our elders, and especially our teachers, with a "yes sir" or "yes ma'am". Older ladies were shown respect by adding a "Miss" in front of their names, and older men were often referred to as "judge", or "squire", especially if he had ever been a justice of the peace or was a large land owner.

My parents adhered to the old rules about children when there were guests. We didn't usually have much company, only a neighbor who might drop in on rare occasions. Our most important company was always the preacher when he would come for Sunday dinner. The old rule, handed down from pioneer days, was that the children should wait until the adults had eaten before being allowed to eat. I remember those long lazy meals my parents, the preacher and his wife, and whomever else my parents had invited from the church would eat, while I took care of the younger children and tried to keep them pacified. My mother always tried to cook plenty, but sometimes, depending on appetites, the best of everything would already have been consumed by the time we got to the table. For many years, I really resented this until once my mother told me about when she was a child and she and her brother would have to wait, and by the time they finally got to eat, there would be nothing left of the Sunday chicken but the feet. A chicken's foot is nothing but bone. My poor mother had really heard it thunder in her lifetime.

The preachers were privileged people in many ways, besides getting the best pieces of the Sunday chicken. When times were hard and money was short, or maybe when it had been a dry summer and the crops were dying, the people sometimes felt that they hadn't been paying the preacher enough. In such a situation, the congregation would sometimes give the preacher a "pounding". A preacher pounding is when each church member brings some comestible (at least a pound of something) for the preacher's larder. This could be a very good thing, but I also knew of some instances when it became both humorous and poignant. We all know that domestic skills vary; some women are good cooks, some are not, some are clever gift givers, some are not. Therefore the preachers never knew what might turn up in a pounding. In one instance of which I became aware, one kindly lady gave the preacher some jars of home-canned blackberries. Evidently, the berries hadn't been properly canned, and on the way home, the jars exploded in the trunk of the preacher's car. I can only imagine the mess they had to deal with.

Manners and morals during the Depression were, as is usually the case, more stringent for women than for men. Most men smoked tobacco and drank alcohol, but it was considered slatternly for a woman to do so. Giggling and laughing were considered unseemly, and slang was frowned upon. Children, except on the playground, were to be seen and not heard. In classrooms, the boys sat on one side, the girls on the other. Girls wore their dresses to below the knees, and with bodices that covered everything above the waist except the arm from the elbows to the hand. With them they wore stockings or knee socks. Ankle socks eventually came in and were called "whoopee socks". They were considered quite daring until people became used to them. A lady always wore a hat and gloves when she went out, even on the warmest summer day. Bathing suits were demure by today's standards, and usually were tank type, skirted affairs that covered well the upper thighs.

It was during this time that women began to "marcel" their hair, and this was considered somewhat scandalous at first. The "marcel" was an early version of the permanent wave, in which the hair was tortured into waves all over the head unrelieved by any hint of a curl except a few "spitcurls" around the face. These were formed by using a gel (or quite often spit) to form a fish-hook curl. Later on, as the Depression began bearing down more and more and the conservative religions became more and more the norm, some women reverted to wearing their hair very long, as women had done in pioneer days. As I understand it, this was based on a scripture from the eleventh chapter of First Corinthians in the Christian Bible. Likewise, some women ceased to wear jewelry, finding it unscriptural. Others, I suspect, had surrendered their trinkets to the pawnbroker. In the case of the dentist's wife, mentioned in an earlier chapter, her husband had melted her gold jewelry down to make fillings for his patients' teeth. Makeup was used sparingly. A bit too much red on lips or cheeks could easily brand one as "loose".

I don't know how the color red ever fell into such disrepute as was its lot during the Depression years. Perhaps it was from the reflected disrepute of the red lights that characterized the bawdyhouses along the coast south of us. Or perhaps it was just that people fell into such a brown funk during the Depression, that anything suggestive of sensuality, joy, or happiness, was automatically considered sinful. Be that as it may, it was considered daring for a woman to wear the least bit of red in her costume during those years. One didn't buy a red coat or a red hat, or heavens forbid, an entire red outfit! It meant that one had slatternly intentions. Furthermore women were captives of these silly codes, no matter how unfair or downright wrong they were because of the fear of being gossiped about. Back then, being gossiped about was the absolute worst thing that could happen to a person, short of death.

During the Depression, a single woman teaching school had to give up her job if she got married, although the same rule did not apply to the men. Our local school lost several teachers who got married and had to leave. Others simply went where they were not known to get married in a simple court house ceremony, and then kept the marriage a secret. This was the breeding ground for several scandals, and of course, the usual gossip. This, of course, was all grossly unfair. I remember one teacher in our acquaintance who came from a large family, of which she was the sole support, while making only forty dollars per month. She married a man, whom she had been dating for years, and they had to keep it secret until the Depression ended and the rule was changed. She was an excellent teacher and to have lost her because of a silly rule would have been a tragedy. None of the couples would have ever considered living together without marriage. That just wasn't done in those days, and a woman was expected to be a virgin when she did get married.

As for sex education, most girls had none. All I was ever told was "keep your dress down". How my mother expected me to ever survive without tragedy, the business of finding a suitable husband, I don't know. But that was the way she had been raised, and that was all she knew. I think the theory was that keeping a girl ignorant was to keep her chaste. That certainly wouldn't work in today's world, and neither was it a very wise plan of action for back then. I think also that the assumption was that I would find out much more than I needed to know from my schoolmates. However, it didn't happen that way, and I grew up incredibly naïve about things I really needed to know. My older sister was no help at all. I always suspected that my mother talked to her, but she never passed any my mother. In my adult life, people have often told me that in some information along to me. Not a word ever came from either her or ways I seem like a little girl. I think they may be right, and I blame it on this part of my upbringing. I resolved that I would never follow that path with my own daughter; that I would err on the side of giving her too much information, if there is such a thing, rather than the other. It's a rough world out there for a girl, and keeping one ignorant is tantamount to making her a social cripple.

My mother had several children during the Depression, but I never knew anything about it until it happened. When my younger sister was born, I came home from school and there she was, in the bed with my mother. I was so glad to have a little girl to take care of, after looking after all boys for so many years. If we weren't at school when the birth occurred, our parents would send us off to one of the neighbors. I remember once, we were sent to our closest neighbor, about a quarter of a mile away, and I thought it strange, that as soon as we entered the house, she ran and changed her apron and was out the door and gone, leaving us with her husband.

Finally she came back and we went home, and sure enough, there was a new baby in the bed with my mother. Evidently, the neighbor had arranged to be with my mother when the time came, and she needed someone to be with her while my father went to town, seven miles away, to get the doctor. I well remember the night my youngest brother was born. I was thirteen years old at the time, and yet didn't know a thing about the impending birth. We kids were roused from bed, all except my older sister, about midnight on Hallowe'en night and sent on a path through the woods to our Aunt's house, about a mile away in the company of another relative. My sister was kept hone to help afterward. I remember walking through the woods in the middle of the night, and not being afraid, only wondering what was going on. There was nothing to be afraid of at that time. We stayed until morning and then went home, to find we had another new sibling. He was the last one, and was everyone's baby, and still is.

After me, my parents never hired any house help when there was a birth. When my oldest brother was born, when I was four years old and my sister was ten, she was in complete charge of cooking the meals and taking care of the family. As I remember, there was an extra person in the household at that time--just a male acquaintance of my father's who had come and put up on us for a few days. I think my father was dealing with him on the purchase of some land. This was a few years before the Depression and my father could afford to buy land. When the next one was born, it was the middle of summer, and dog days were upon us. It rained steady for three weeks, and we couldn't get any laundry done. When the baby was born, he had an eye infection and then scratched himself in the eye, and my mother was terrified that he would be blind. Then, just when it seemed nothing else could possibly happen, one of my mother's breasts became infected and she went through a terrible time with that for about two months. It was just a terrible time for all of us, but especially for my sister and me.

Our final two siblings were both born in October and my sister stayed out of school both times and took care of the house and our mother. I remember that when the last one was born, the tale was told at school that my sister had had a baby. Somehow, we survived all of it.

Even with all the conservative religion and the strict code of morals and mores, I don't know if people were really any more moral back then than they are now. On the surface, it would certainly seem so. However, I remember that it was very common to find a used condom on the school grounds in the morning, although at the time I had not the foggiest idea of what it was. I never did know until after I grew up. I also remember my father talking about the dirty politics that were going on in town, and at the state capitol. No, I don't think people were any more moral. People are just people, imperfect creatures, no matter what their circumstance.

One thing that happened when I was about thirteen or fourteen I have never understood. One day, just out of the blue, my mother said "you're going to stay home until you learn how to act". I didn't know then, she didn't explain, and to this day I don't know what I had done to precipitate such a verdict. But she stuck to her word. From then until I left home, I never went anywhere except to church and to school, and now and then a Sunday school party. I never was allowed to date, although my sister began dating when she was sixteen. I was a different type to my sister, and I think my parents took that as a challenge. I was also extremely quiet when I was growing up. My mother often remarked on it later, after I was grown up and became my own person, and somewhat loquacious.

I would not end this chapter, which is meant to be about manners and morals without mentioning one thing that my father was very, very strict about. I suppose it was an echo of his backwoods upbringing and hard times that he always rode herd on the kids at mealtime, and admonished us about taking a larger helping of food on our plates than we could eat. We would come in from working in the field or whatever, and so hungry we thought we could eat one of the cows, hooves and all. In that kind of a situation, it is very easy to take more on one's plate than one can eat. However, our father was always there to see that we didn't. Both our parents thought it a sin to be wasteful. Of course, in our house nothing was ever wasted, since what the family didn't consume went to either the dogs or the hogs, Nevertheless, our father never failed to admonish us when we took more than what could be considered a normal helping of food on our plates. This particular thing was, I think, concerned with both manners and morals.

X

Kerosene, Turpentine and Dry Mustard

During the Great Depression, our family; could not afford medical care, so a doctor was called only for the birth of a baby or if a situation was considered really life-threatening. I don't remember ever being at the doctor's office after about age four until I was about sixteen. When I was about four, I stepped barefooted into a pile of burning sawdust at the site where a sawmill had once been. One of my feet was burned so badly I had to be taken to the doctor twice. After that, I didn't see a doctor again for many years. When I turned thirteen, however, my face broke out with terrible acne. This continued all through my teens. I also walked in my sleep. I think now that both these things were the result of the stress in my life, since immediately after I left home and went away to college, my face cleared, and I never walked in my sleep again. When I was about sixteen, and my acne was worse than any I have seen since, I made a trip to the doctor. My sister and I were making a rare trip to town one day, and my mother told my sister that she could take me to the doctor's office, and possibly get something for it.

When we reached the doctor's office, he took a look at my face and said the breaking out was caused by consuming too much sugar. I knew it wasn't true, but he was the doctor. He gave me a small bottle of medicine called phenolthalein and told me to take five drops a day. I have since learned that phenolthalein is the main ingredient in many laxatives. I took the five drops daily religiously until the bottle was empty, and my acne not only didn't improve, but if anything, became worse. It only improved when I went away to college and got out of the environment in which I had grown up and that I hated so much.

I relate this only to illustrate that we did not visit doctors' offices with any frequency back then. My oldest brother caught diphtheria when he was about eight years old, and we were quarantined one whole summer, and of course this required a doctor. Then my third brother got pneumonia and was delirious one winter, and our parents had a doctor for him. Generally speaking, however, the doctor came only when there was a baby to be delivered. My mother did the most of the doctoring.

As I look back on it from the vantage-point of many years, I realize that our parents probably denied us many activities that we would have enjoyed. This was to avoid the doctor bills that would have resulted from an injury. There simply wasn't any money for doctor bills. I never learned to swim, although there were several creeks nearby. I never learned to ride a horse, although we owned one. The boys never played football because my father flatly forbade it. We all missed out on some things that would have enriched our lives.

One of my great-great grandmothers on my mother's side of the family was a Cherokee plant woman. I was told years ago by people who were old enough to have known her that she spent much of her time in the woods, searching for plants, berries, and roots, from which to make medicines. My mother's heritage must have drawn heavily from this slice of her gene pool, for she loved the woods, and loved to find remedies for her family's ailments among the plants and trees. Many times, I saw her boil red oak bark to soak and infected foot or hand. She used pokeroot much the same way. Having lived in the woods all during her growing up years, and raised in the home of her adopted grandfather, who had fought in the Indian Wars and was well versed in the Indian ways, she had a working knowledge of what plants were good for medicine, and which ones weren't. She also used many remedies that were handed down from the pioneers. The one we all remember best was her "tanky bags", a name we kids gave to this particular remedy. She would take a few spoonfuls of turpentine, add an equal amount of kerosene, soak a flannel cloth in the mixture, and place it across the chest of whichever one of us was coming down with a chest cold. It always worked, but oh, how it would stink!

Speaking of remedies that are odoriferous, one thing our mother never inflicted on us was asafetida. Asafetida is a brown, resinous, very offensive smelling material derived from fennel plants. In olden days, it was widely used as a medicine. Almost every child in the old one-room schoolhouses would wear a small wad of the stuff wrapped on a bit of cloth and tied around their neck, to ward off all kinds of illnesses, especially any illness pertaining to the upper respiratory system. Our mother had had to endure this indignity in her kid-hood, but luckily other medicines had been introduced before she had children, so we escaped. I don't remember ever smelling asafetida but once, but it is a smell so unbelievably offensive you never forget it.

Another favorite remedy of my mother was a mustard plaster. This was made by wetting a few spoonfuls of dry mustard with a bit of water, spreading it on a flannel cloth, folding the cloth to form a poultice, and placing the poultice across the patient's chest. I have had my chest blistered many times by a mustard plaster, but they always worked. In fact my mother's mustard plaster remedy probably saved my life when I was only three months old and had bi-polar pneumonia and whooping cough simultaneously. They had a trained nurse who lived in the community to come and take care of me for some time, and the doctor came every day. Finally the doctor gave up on me and told my parents there was nothing they could do for me then but buy a little white casket. This must have nearly killed my parents, who had not long since lost one of their children in the flu epidemic of 1918. After hearing the doctor's verdict, the nurse asked my mother if there was anything more she would like her to do. My mother said "yes, put on one more mustard plaster", which the nurse did. Soon afterward, I began to recover, and my mother always credited my recovery to the mustard plasters.

In the summertime, we were always covered with insect bites. If we went into the woods or blackberry patches picking berries, we always became covered with red bugs. Red bugs are tiny little insects, no larger than a pinpoint, bright red in color, and very, very poisonous. The welts from their bites can remain and continue to itch for months. The remedy at our house was to touch each bug bite with a drop of laundry bleach. Ticks were also a big problem in the woods and fields. The remedy for this was to change our clothes and launder them as soon as possible, before the ticks travel to various parts of the house install themselves in the crevices and begin multiplying. Once they do this, getting rid of them is a complicated and expensive process. After dealing with our tick-ridden clothes, we had to check our skin to make sure no tick had "seized up" anywhere. When a tick "seizes up", it sinks its pincers into the skins so firmly that removing them tears their heads off. If not detected and removed, they will sit there and suck blood for weeks, until they fall off. Bathing will not remove them. When they finally fall off, they break open and produce dozens of little ticks.

Fire ants were also a problem. If one happens to step into a fire-ant bed in the dark, as I did once, one can easily be covered from head to foot in a few seconds. A fire-ant bite doesn't just itch: it also festers and makes an eruption in the skin. Fire ant bites are also extremely painful. The remedy in our household was to get the ants off one's self as fast as possible, then dab each bite with a bit of laundry bleach, just as with the red bugs.

None of us ever was bitten by a snake, which is something of a miracle, considering the amount of time we all spent in the woods. The reason we were so fortunate probably was because we always had several dogs about the place, and if we went into the woods the dogs were always with us. If one of us had ever been bitten, it would have required a visit to a doctor or an emergency room.

Everyone went barefoot in the summer, and a major danger was that we might step on a nail or a shard of glass. This happened with some regularity. These wounds were treated with iodine and bandaged with a clean white cloth. This treatment was routine for such things as stubbed toes, cut fingers, and skinned knees. One of the worst wounds I remember from that era was when my sister ran into an old rusty plowshare hidden in some weeds that had grown up around it and sliced her leg very badly. Her wound got the usual treatment--iodine and a bandage. Another time, my sister and I were digging worms for fishing. She was wielding the grubbing hoe while I was retrieving the worms and putting them into a can. In my enthusiasm I got in the way of her hoe and was hit a pretty good lick in the forehead. I didn't suffer any permanent damage, but it gave my parents a bad scare.

As mentioned elsewhere, my father always butchered, so our dogs always had plenty of bones on which to chew. There were always beef bones lying about the back yard. One day, when I was about twelve, and was at my usual job of minding the younger ones, my oldest brother, who would have been about eight, became perturbed with me for some reason. His reaction was to pick up a jawbone of a cow that was lying in the yard, and hurling it at me, striking me on the forehead just above my left eye. I still have the scar from that encounter. The wound was treated with the usual iodine and a bandage.

My father was a great believer in medicating with whiskey, especially if the illness had anything to do with the upper respiratory tract. He had suffered from pneumonia several times, and I suppose thought that if it was good for him, it should be recommended for everyone. Any way, I remember once, when I was about ten years old and had the flu, my parents gave me a drink that tasted rather awful, and they were mysterious about it, not telling me what it was. I think it was whiskey with honey and lemon, but good back- sliding Methodists that they were, they couldn't tell me that. I think the whiskey must have been bottled in bond, since it was a brownish color. Wildcat whiskey is colorless.

I suppose the absolute worst medical emergency that ever happened at our house was in 1934. My younger sister was three years old at the time. One day my father was sitting in front of the fireplace with his legs stretched out across the hearth, warming his feet, my sister darted across the hearth, stumbled over his feet, and fell into the bed of red-hot coals in the fireplace. My father grabbed her as fast as he could, but the back of her head was burned very badly, and of course, her hair all gone. I remember coming home from school that day, my mother telling me of the accident, and taking me to the bed where she was sleeping and showing me show badly her head was burned. It broke my heart, for I was so proud of my baby sister, after babysitting so many boys for so many years. They hadn't taken her to the doctor, thinking no doubt that there wasn't much he could do that they couldn't do.

My mother doctored her according to what she knew. We were so afraid that the burn was so deep that her hair would never grow back, but eventually, over several years it did grow back as thick as ever. The texture wasn't the same as the rest of her hair for a while, but eventually that righted itself also. In high school, my younger sister was one of the school beauties, a status neither my older sister nor I ever attained.

My mother believed in spring tonics. One of her favorites was sulfur. She would mix a dose (maybe a half teaspoonful) with a spoonful of syrup, making it easier for the hapless recipient to swallow the mess. Another so-called tonic that I remember was calomel. I don't remember the others ever being given calomel, but I got a round of calomel every spring. My mother said that when one took calomel one couldn't eat, since it would salivate you. To this day, I don't know what that means. I assume that "salivate" is a derivative of the word "saliva", but how could salivating portend the deadly end that was intimated. One day when I had been taking calomel and was so hungry I could have eaten a rag doll, I just happened to be in the house alone, and there just happened to be a bowl of fried corn sitting on the table. I tasted it, and it was so good that like Goldilocks, I ate it all. When my mother returned she wanted to know what happened to the corn. When I told her I ate it, I was afraid that she would kill me, and I wouldn't have to worry about being salivated. She was majorly dismayed, but said very little.

The usual assortment of old fashioned remedies always sat on the shelf at our house. There was castor oil, carbolated vaseline and black draught (senna) for the older children, and paregoric, and syrup of figs for the infants and toddlers. However, my mother's home remedies were the ones that really saw us through our childhood--that and the good fresh vegetables we always ate. Considering our lack of access to doctors, and the doctors' lack of sophistication, it was only through her knowledge and her diligence that we all grew up healthy.

XI

General Beauregard and New Year's Gifts

When I was a child, the various holidays of the year were not noted and celebrated in the manner or with the intensity that they are today. People were far too poor to spend money on celebrations. Birthdays were generally ignored in our family, as I suspect they were in most of the families we knew. Today, some people try to ignore their birthdays, not wishing to dwell on the subject of their age, but back then, it was economics, pure and simple.

At that time this was long before MLK day became a holiday, the first holiday noted on the calendar was Groundhog Day, which was and is February second. The legend, handed down from our agrarian ancestors that if the sun shines that day, in other words, if the groundhog sees his shadow, there will be six more weeks of winter. Down south this unreliable little weather prognosticator is called General Beauregard. Up north he is known as Punxatawney Phil. Groundhog Day is merely a fun holiday, apparently put into the calendar as a nod to history and to furnish a photo op for the newspeople who go out and take pictures of the furry little critter after he is dragged out of his den. We never paid any particular attention to Groundhog Day, knowing that planting time was just around the corner regardless.

Valentine's Day was not a very big deal, either. The children exchanged valentines at school. The ones I gave, when I gave any at all, were always home made. Therefore, the few I received were also homemade, since, children being what they are, no one wanted to give a pretty store bought valentine and receive a homemade one in return. There was also many hurts attendant to this practice. Some children would receive dozens of valentines and some very few or none at all. Today the schools have abandoned this practice, and if a child gives a valentine to one, they have to give to everyone in the class. I applaud this practice. Hurting a child is a terrible thing.

Among the teens and twenty-somethings, candy and flowers were the usual valentine gifts, just as they are today. Occasionally someone would give a valentine party, but this wasn't very often, since dancing was frowned upon, and spin-the-bottle type games were disdained, leaving little to do at a party. Social drinking had not yet arrived in this part of the country. There was plenty of drinking, mind you, but it was usually done in the woodshed, from a crockery jug.

Saint Patrick's Day was never celebrated in our part of the country. I never ever knew there was such a holiday until long after I had grown up and left home. I suppose it was because we didn't have many residents of Irish ancestry. We had many Scotch-Irish, but that is something different.

May Day was usually celebrated at school. Perhaps this was a throwback to the Celtic background of most of the students at that time. It is another custom that has died out as our country has become more and more multi-cultural. On the first day of May, we would have a celebration outdoors in the form of songs, dances, and recitals. I remember once, I was part of a maypole dance, which I thought was very pretty. It's all just a part of our history now.

Easter, being one of the holiest days in the Christian calendar, was always celebrated as befitted its importance. All the women who could afford it bought a new outfit, or at least a new hat, for Easter, and always a new dress and slippers for their daughters. It was a very pretty sight on Easter morning, to see them at church wearing their pastel outfits. Sometimes we could afford a few yards of cotton material for Easter dresses, but more than likely not.

Dying Easter eggs was always a thing we enjoyed at our house. I would go into the woods and gather what we called "egg dye", and never knew the botanical name. This I would boil along with the eggs, and they would come out a very pretty yellow color. Other eggs I would put into the coffee pot and boil along with the coffee. These would come out tan. Others we would dye by wrapping them in scraps of wet crepe paper in various colors while they were still hot. We had to dye enough eggs that each one of us who was of school age would have at least three eggs to take to school for the egg hunt. That would be on Friday. Then on Sunday there would be another egg hunt just for the family. I always enjoyed Easter, especially dying the eggs and hiding them for the younger children. We always had plenty of eggs, and with our creative ways of dying them, this holiday didn't present the financial challenge that some of the others did.

Mothers' Day, on the other hand, always presented a challenge. We never had a dime to buy anything for our mother, who was the most deserving person I have ever known. I tried to make it up to her after getting out on my own. That was all I could do. Mothers' Day usually fell on the same day as Memorial Day at the local Baptist church Cemetery where my mother's ancestors were buried. It had been the custom since the cemetery was established in the late eighteen hundreds to have dinner on the ground at the church on Memorial Day. Each family would bring a basket of food and a cloth which would be spread on the ground for a communal meal. My mother always enjoyed attending these affairs and seeing the people she had grown up with. This custom has died out now.

Another custom associated with Mothers' Day that has died out was the wearing of flowers in honor of your mother. If your mother was among the living, it was proper to wear a red flower (preferably a rose) in her honor on Mothers' Day. If she was deceased, you wore a white flower. I think we have lost a great deal with the passage of this custom. A poignant memory that sticks in my mind is of a young sailor in San Diego during World War II, far from home, far from his mother, but wearing, in her honor, a very beautiful red rose in a nest of baby's breath fern pinned to his uniform. The colors were so pretty--the beautiful red rose against the blue and white of the sailor's uniform, topped by his innocent face. I only saw him briefly, and never knew his name, but I have never forgotten him.

The Fourth of July was always a fun time for us during the Depression, because we had all the things required except firecrackers, and no one else had firecrackers, so we didn't miss them. We usually had watermelons and cantaloupes at that time of the year. Sometimes, but not always, our father would get a goat for barbecuing. Then someone would stay up all night attending the barbecue, and keeping it basted with the sweet and sour tomato sauce we always used. We usually could afford this kind of a celebration, even during the Depression, since a goat only cost two or three dollars. In my earliest memories there had been a picnic at the church every Fourth of July. However, there eventually were so many non-members coming just for the food that the church could no longer afford it.

Labor Day was not celebrated in our part of the country during the Depression. The labor movement had not gained strength in the south at that time, and I don't recall that there were ever any parades or other celebrations to mark the day.

Hallowe'en was very different in those days. Today it seems to be a holiday mostly for the children. Back then, however, there was no "trick or treating". Rather, it was a night of mischief, done usually by the older boys and young men of the community. They did such things as overturning privies, smearing car windows with soap, throwing eggs (preferably rotten ones) at certain houses, and painting graffiti with a paint brush rather than a spray can, as would be done today. Most people took it good naturedly, repaired the damage, and didn't complain. In school, we drew jack-o-lanterns,, black cats, bats, and witches, which the teacher would display on the windows of the schoolhouse, or along the blackboard.

Sometimes there would be a Hallowe'en festival at the school on Hallowe'en night, and everyone in the community would come. There usually would be a play, presented by one of the classes, and each class would sponsor a merchandising project to earn money for the school. There would be hot dogs with pickles, kraut, mustard and ketchup for a nickel apiece, ice cream cones for a nickel apiece, home made candy and cookies for a nickel per serving. It was not wise to ask for more than a nickel for anything, since no one had any money.

Thanksgiving was a very solemn celebration. People were encouraged to go to church on that day to give thanks. Families gathered for the noonday meal, but it was not always a feast, as it is likely to be today. Many families sat down to a meal of beans and cornbread on Thanksgiving Day. Our family usually had some kind of fowl, either chicken or duck and later Turkey, after we began raising them. In the afternoon, the men usually went hunting, the women visited, and when the day was over, Thanksgiving was over. It didn't stretch out into a four-day mini vacation as it often does today.

Christmas, the brightest holiday of the year, was a very sad time for many people during the Great Depression. Before the Depression descended upon us, we had always had a fairly nice Christmas, with gifts and treats. Our father usually would bring a crate of the very best oranges and a crate of red delicious apples from town on Christmas Eve. We would have cakes and candy and anything we wanted to eat. In the dark days of the Depression, however, this all changed or ended altogether. Sometimes we got no fruit at all for Christmas. Other times my father would bring home one bag (maybe two dozen) of apples and another of oranges.

There was never any candy, cookies, or cakes, except what my sister and I made. This was no great handicap since our father always bought sugar a hundred pounds at a time, so we always had plenty of sugar and flour, cocoa, butter, and eggs, for making cakes and candies. Also, my sister and I both liked to cook sweets, so we usually had plenty. Christmas dinner was more or less a duplication of what we had had for Thanksgiving, just good farm food. This was reason to be ever thankful for our good fortune, since there were so many people had nothing except what was given them at the social welfare office.

We always had a Christmas tree. We would go into the woods with an axe, search for a well-shaped young pine tree and chop it down, and drag it home. With two end pieces of ceiling a few nails and a hammer, we would fashion a pedestal, and were ready to decorate. We never had any store- bought ornaments. The seed balls from a sweet gum tree covered with the tin-foil inner wrappings of cigarette packages (picked up along the roadsides all year long) made great ornaments. Also small gifts from school were hung directly on the tree and did double duty as ornaments. Then we made paper chains, and popcorn strings to finish the decorating. We usually had a very pretty tree. We usually could find plentiful mistletoe and holly with berries in the woods roundabout, to decorate the rest of the house.

As for gifts, we got nothing. There just was no money for gifts. We would draw names at school, and somehow manage to get a ten-cent gift for the person whose name we drew, and conversely receive a similar in value gift from the person who drew our name. This usually was all we got for Christmas. I remember how perturbed I used to get at my mother when people would ask me what I get for Christmas, and I would reply "nothing". My mother would always say, "but you got so and so", and name the small gift I had received at school. As I look back on it now, I should have been perturbed at the person who dared to ask such a rude question, especially in such hard times, rather than at my mother. Both our mother and our father had known extremely hard times in their early life, and knew how to appreciate even the smallest gift. My father once told me that as a child he hung up his stocking faithfully year after year after year, all through his childhood and never was rewarded with even a stick of candy. Knowing her history, I suspect that my mother fared equally poorly.

Back to the subject of the school gifts, I can remember a few Christmases when we couldn't even afford the few dimes it took to buy the presents for our gift exchanges at school. In these instances, my sister made chocolate fudge, and we would each give our gift person a good-sized package of it. It went over well.

Some students, however, couldn't even afford that. I remember one Christmas when I was in high school, my good friend whom I write about in another chapter, happened to draw my name. I had been desperately looking forward to my school gift, knowing that it was all I would get for Christmas. Finally, the morning came and we all exchanged presents. When I opened the box from my friend, I found only a few dry pods of peas and a note that said "eat me and have a swell Christmas". It was just a little joke, since peas, like other legumes are notorious for causing flatulence. I was so hurt I couldn't even cry, though I tried not to let her know it. She seemed so sheepish; I knew she was as embarrassed as I was.

One quaint Christmas custom that I think I am glad has died out was the custom of yelling "Christmas gift," when you first saw a person at Christmas time. No matter how inappropriate you might think this to be, you didn't dare not do it, because if the other person got "Christmas gift" on you first, you had to give him or her a gift instead of getting one yourself. I have known of people giving away gifts they had only just received because they felt obligated in this childish game. This custom was repeated again at New Year's. If someone yelled "New Year's gift" instead of "Hello" when they saw you, you were obliged to give them a gift. Many people routinely gave New Year's gifts back then, especially to individuals from whom they had received Christmas gifts, but to whom they had not given anything, but doing it this way was really tacky. I suppose it was a characteristic of the hard times through which we were living that people would more or less "ask" for gifts in this way, but I'm glad that this tradition was left behind in the detritus of the Great Depression.

The only other way I remember New Year's being celebrated during that dark period was the blowing of the work whistles at the mines and mills in town, seven miles away at midnight on New Year's Eve. Nearer at hand, people would blast with their shot guns or set off dynamite. Even though we didn't have any close neighbors. We could hear the commotion from miles away.

Whether New Year's Eve or any other time, a favorite activity of some of the rough types who lived up the road from us, seemed to be shooting at our mailbox. Their courage bolstered by a few shots of wildcat whiskey, they loved to use our mailbox for target practice. We had several new boxes over the years, but a bright shiny new mailbox only seemed to encourage the rabble-rousers. When it rained, we always had damp mail because of the bullet holes. This had never happened when the mailboxes were all bunched together on the lonely stretch of road some distance from our house--only after the route was changed and the box moved and situated right in front of our house. I think the shootings were meant as a personal affront to the family, but the perpetrator was too cowardly to do any more than shoot our poor inanimate mailbox.

Birthdays were not given any special significance at our house. If someone was having a birthday, our mother would try to cook a something special for our noonday meal, but there was no birthday cake or presents. This never seemed to matter to any of us. We had to work on our birthdays the same as any other day. We were trying to survive in a world that had turned very harsh, and anything as self-oriented as a birthday was no incentive for celebration

XII

Good Times Are Where You Find Them

Despite the pall that hung over our country during the Depression, people desperately tried to have fun. However, in our family, there was not much fun to be had except the fun that we made for ourselves. As I remember, most of the enjoyment I experienced during those years came from the woods and nature around us. I liked nothing better than to go berry picking. Even though the blackberry thorns were brutal to our hands, It was a happy day for me when I could spend it in the blackberry patch oblivious to the snakes, redbugs, and ticks. I also liked picking huckleberries, but by the time of the Great Depression, most of the huckleberries had been killed off by the forest fires. I do remember once going huckleberry picking on Bluff Ridge with my grandfather, just the two of us. I suppose those few hours were the longest time I ever spent with my grandfather alone. We didn't find many huckleberries that day, but we talked, and he showed me the route he used to take as a child across Bluff Ridge as he walked the six miles he had to walk through dense woods to school each day as a child. It made me realize that, hard as times were at the moment, our family was very fortunate, compared with the lives our forbears had lived.

I loved roaming the woods to see what could be found that was edible. I would eat "possum grapes and muscadines. "Possum grapes" are small wild grapes that grow on ambitious vines that reach to the top of the trees. Opossums love to eat them. Muscadines are large blue grapes that are very tasty to eat, and make wonderful jellies and preserves. The golden colored version of the same fruit, known as scuppernongs, has been grown in back yard arbors since colonial times, and can be bought in many stores today. I also loved black haws, wild plums, paw-paws, maypops, and especially wild persimmons. I still love wild persimmons, but seldom see any these days.

My favorite by far of all the things foraged from the woods was hickory nuts. I dearly loved hickory nuts. I would gather them by the bushels (literally), and crack them at night when we were sitting by the fire. My father would often complain about the hickory nut shells that he stepped on with his bare feet when he arose in the morning. My sister and I would also crack and pick large amounts of hickory nut meats to put in candy and cakes. I especially liked the kind that we called "scaly barks". "Scaly barks were a kind of hickory nuts that grew in swampy places, one of which was right in front of our house, and eventually was acquired and became part of our homestead. The shells of "scaly barks" were thin, and the nut meats very sweet, so we gathered those any time we could.

I suppose the thing we enjoyed the most as a group was fishing. There was a creek just down the hill from our house, and as it meandered through one of our fields between the road and the railroad, another stream flowed into it and there were some deep holes that were good for fishing. In the summertime we would often go fishing at night after all the work was done. What we caught was mostly yellow perch and catfish, but I suppose catching fish wasn't really the point. We enjoyed being out on the creek among nature. There was nothing to be afraid of, ever. I remember once we were fishing late at night at a place we called the "old mill pond". It was in the woods, at a place where my grandfather and great uncle had once long ago dammed the stream to build a grist mill. The dam was still there, and the backwaters made an excellent fishing hole. We were fishing rather late into the night when my sister got a rather insistent bite on her line. Pulling it up, she discovered it was only a crawdad, but with all those wiggly legs and swinging back and forth toward her, it unnerved her so that she fell into the millpond. We had a good laugh on her, and of course she was so vexed and nonplussed, and don't forget wet, we had to go home after that.

We never went to movies. I saw my first movie when I was about sixteen. I still remember, the name of it was "Saturday's Millions", and I think the star was Ray Milland, but I'm not entirely clear on that. I didn't get to see another one until I grew up and was away from home. My sister went on movie dates, but I never dated as long as I was at home. People thought up many kinds of homespun activities to foster some kind of social life. If someone had a particularly good crop of watermelons, they might host a watermelon cutting. This was long before watermelons had been hybridized into the small, round variety we often see today. They didn't have to fit into a refrigerator, because people didn't have refrigerators. Farmers prided themselves on growing very large melons, and when one was invited to a watermelon cutting, they would see a very large pile of very large melons. Someone would cut them with a huge knife, as they were needed, and each person would be given a half watermelon. That was so that each person could have some of the sweet center-meat of the melon, and not just the less tasty part nearer the rind. Next day the hogs would feast on what was left after the humans finished.

Sometimes, if one could afford it, they might host a chili supper. The nearest equivalent to this today would be the ham and bean suppers or the corned beef and cabbage suppers that some churches sponsor to raise money. People would just gather and eat chili and socialize. Much of our social life was right at home, perhaps with one or two other people, perhaps not. After the fall harvest was in, we would always have peanuts, and sometimes popcorn, if we had raised any that year, and we always had sorghum molasses. We would make molasses taffy and have candy pullings, pop popcorn and make popcorn balls, or just parch a pan full of peanuts. Those were good times.

Once in a while our Sunday school class would have a party or function of some kind. I remember once, we had a swimming party at a swimming hole someone knew about. Mostly our parties were just dull affairs where we played dull games and were served cake and peaches. I never enjoyed these events, since the same snobbishness and mean spiritedness existed here as existed at church. One thing that I did enjoy was singing. In fact, everyone did back then. People would sing as they worked in the fields, or did their housework, or as they walked along the road. During this period, one of my mother's sisters who lived not far from us would host a "singing" several times a year. Those who attended, all except my sister and me, were from the Baptist community, and they loved to sing. Someone (I don't remember who) would play the piano, and we would sing our hearts out, using the Baptist hymnal, which was new and interesting to us, since we were Methodists.

Sometimes one of the churches would hold a cakewalk or a box supper to raise money. These were worthwhile diversions. The most often used format, however, was a "tacky party". At that time, everyone was so poor; choosing an outfit for a tacky party was no problem. You simply picked the ugliest, most out of date, ill fitting, mismatched garments you could find, put them on and go. They always gave a prize for the tackiest outfit. All in all, however, those years were a very lonely, frustrating time for me. One bright spot was an elderly couple who lived about a quarter of a mile away from us, and were our nearest neighbors. They were extremely poor, but in love and kindness, they were very rich indeed. All of our grandparents had died before we were born, except my mother's father, and because of family circumstances, we rarely saw him. This elderly couple made up for it to a great extent. We were always welcome in their home, and they always gave us some kind of a treat, a piece of fruit, a slice of watermelon or cantaloupe, or some nuts that he had found in the woods. Once he gave me a gold mechanical pencil that he had found on the street in town. It must have been worth quite a bit, and much to my sorrow, it disappeared when I went away to college. Neither of them could read or write and he knew that I was doing well in school, so I was the lucky recipient. To all of us, they were the grandparents we never had, and did as much as anyone to brighten my lonely childhood.

I never had any friends my own age, except my school friends, and they were only friends at school. I never saw them outside of school, except sometimes at church. Among my school friends, I had one special friend all through grade and secondary school. She came to our school when I was in the second grade. I well remember that morning. Her grandmother, an elderly woman with her hair in a knot on the top of her head, and wearing a long dress sweeping the tops of her shoes, came to our school with four children, three boys and one girl. The girl became my friend, and remained so until her death.

In all the years that I knew my friend, I never knew what had happened in the family to precipitate their coming to live with their grandparents. They were very private people. Anyway, the girl and I became friends from the very first day. She was smart as a whip. Up until then, I had been the star pupil in my class, but now everyone said we had two.

We were friends on through grade school, and in the seventh grade, were transferred to the consolidated high school about six miles away. There, we were both put into an advanced class and made two grades that year. The five years from then until graduation, we were always together at school, taking the same classes, keeping to the same schedule. She was a very quiet girl, never making any waves at school. I am sure, as I look back on it now, that there were many times that she was hungry, but I don't remember her ever complaining about anything, either her lack of clothes, of spending money, or the bleak life she led in the home of her grandparents. She never brought a lunch to school, but then neither did I, although I suspect it may have been for different reasons. My reason was that I was ashamed to take biscuits, and my father never bought sliced bread. She did have one advantage over me in that she had plenty of time to study, and someone to help her with her studies. She had an uncle who also lived at the home of her grandparents, but in a small building separate from the house. There he always had a fire going at night in the winter, and my friend could go there and study away from the noise of the household, and he would help her with her studies. From all she told me of him, he must have been a really good man. However, in our senior year he died of brain cancer.

After high school I went away to college, and my friend was soon offered a job in Washington, D.C. I never saw her much after that, but we kept in touch by letters. She told me she was engaged to a captain in the army, and a wedding was imminent. Then, when she didn't say any more about it for a while, I asked her and she said that she had gone to visit his family one weekend, and that his mother had then broken them up. She didn't consider my friend pretty enough or sophisticated enough to make a suitable wife for her son. Actually, she was a very lovely girl, and a very good girl. But mothers were like that about their sons back then. If one came from the country that was also always a black mark. City people back then just thought they were better than country people, and it was evident everywhere. I encountered it many times in my own life, but thankfully, not in the choosing of a mate. My friend eventually married another man, a "second choice" type. She died at a fairly young age, as did her three brothers. Her influence on my young life was immeasurable, and it was all good.

No, the Depression years were not fun, except such fun as we made for ourselves, and the few good friends that blessed our paths. However, they were innocent years, by today's standards. There were no drugs, no organized street gangs, and no school shootings. I think perhaps that we were the unknowing recipients of good luck encased in a very cruel package of poverty, deprivation, and the mean spiritedness of un-evolved humans

XIII

Ghost Stories and True Crime

I remember as a child sitting around the fire at night and listening to ghost stories. Everyone, it seemed, had at least one. My grandfather's story of meeting a ghostly night rider at Prince Crossing has already been touched on in another chapter. An even scarier story, this one true, concerns my grandfather when he was a young man. At the time, he was working on a crew laying out the streets of Bessemer, when the town was brand new. He always rode a horse the seven miles to work. My great grandfather owned blooded saddle horses, the result of some trading he did with northern soldiers during the Civil War. The soldiers camped on Cahaba River, a few miles from the old homestead. My great grandfather would go to their camp under cover of darkness and trade horses--a well-fed, well-rested farm horse for a blooded, but almost-ridden-to-death purebred they had looted from some plantation on the Tennessee River in northern Alabama. He would take his purebreds home, feed them well and let them rest, and soon he had the finest horses in the country.

On the night this story happened, my grandfather was riding one of my great grandfather's horses, coming home from his job. It was payday, and he had his pay in his pocket. About halfway home, at a spot where the road paralleled Shades Creek (I know the exact spot), some men way laid him, no doubt intending to take his money and possibly kill him, but the intelligence of the horse saved his life. The horse knew the men were there long before my grandfather heard or saw them, and when they jumped out from the trees to attack, the horse took one great leap and was gone, saving my grandfather from a very nasty incident.

My mother loved to tell the story of my great great grandfather's narrow escapes as he was migrating to Alabama from Clarksville, Tennessee. The family came down the Cumberland River on a raft to Nashville, and then overland to the vicinity of present day Bessemer. She told of near drownings in the Cumberland River, and then in the Tennessee River, which they had to cross in Northern Alabama. She told of my great grandfather being swept off his swimming horse, in the swollen Tennessee, and having to hang onto some brush all night in mid river, until he could be rescued. She told of his waking up in the middle of the night, as the family camped, and seeing a man with a knife raised, ready to cut his throat. She told of highwaymen jumping onto their loaded wagons and throwing things off to go back and gather up later. Being far outnumbered, all they could do was urge the horses on, keep moving, and pretend they didn't know they were being robbed.

Both my mother's and my father's ancestors had come into the Alabama Territory while the Indians still roamed the woods. The woods were so dense back then, and the trees so large, my mother said that even when she was a child, one could be walking in the woods, get a glimpse of someone maybe thirty yards away, and they might dart behind a tree, never to be seen again, no matter how hard you might look. When one neighbor couple moved onto a tract of land near my great grandfather's tract, they found a dead man sitting, leaning against a large tree. They never knew who he was or what had caused his death, but reasoned that a highland moccasin or a rattlesnake may have bitten him.

Then there were stories of happenings that weren't really crimes, but were cause for wonderment. For instance one man that we knew spent his entire life trying to unravel the mystery of what happened to his father. His father had gone away one day and just never came back. I don't think this had been all that unusual at one period in our history when divorce was uncommon. If a couple were having marital problems, rather than bother getting a dissolution of the marriage, the man quite often would just hitch up the wagon, click to the horse, and be gone, never to be heard from again.

My mother told the story of a neighbor family she knew when she was growing up. In fact the man of the family had married one of her distant relatives. When the Civil War came, he had gone away to war, and while he was away his wife had gotten cozy with her brother-in-law, (her sister's husband), and became pregnant by him. When her husband heard about it, he sent word for her not to be in his home when he returned. The wife then went to live with her sister and her brother-in-law by whom she eventually had another child. These were people we had not known, but our ancestors had.

During the Depression, we still listened to ghost stories and folklore, but there also was a prolific collection of real crime stories. Most of it was a by-product of the illegal distillation of corn whiskey in the hollows round about. I have mentioned several times the Celtic sense of humor that runs strong in the southern psyche. The flip side of that is a quick, fiery temper. Many of the people of that time had a very short fuse. Couple this with the consumption of alcohol distilled in the woods and containing who knows what impurities and tragic things can happen. They quite often happened among relatives. One incident we all knew about involved two neighbors who were married to sisters. They had had a disagreement and the one man went riding up to the other's porch on his horse, perhaps to seek peace. The response of his brother-in-law who lived in the house was to shoot him off his horse.

Another such incident involved a man in the community who shot and killed a neighbor in a drunken disagreement. Then some months later, the dead man's wife's brother took up the fight and killed the first man who was known to be a "smart Alec", and had taunted him with the words, "one of us is going to wake up in hell tonight."

My mother told the story of a man who lived on Pine Mountain. He often furnished lodging for overnight travelers who happened to be caught on the road when darkness fell. Everyone knew that he did this, and so they wondered why they could sometimes look across late at night and see the light of a torch progressing along the crest of the lonely mountain. They wondered if it was their neighbor up there, what task he was about, and if one of his overnight guests had come to some harm. Back then it was fairly common for a person to offer lodging to a wayfarer and then rob and murder him. No one ever knew, of course.

Perhaps the most poignant tale concerned a well-respected citizen of another community, who had three daughters. As the daughters grew into womanhood, there were no social outlets for them in the lonely area where they lived. As it happened, the man had hired a young black man to help with the farm work, and as it also happened, the youngest of the four daughters began engaging in secret trysts with the black man and subsequently became pregnant. The black man promptly took off for parts unknown. When the father learned of his daughter's condition, he was enraged, but finally told her she could go ahead and have the child but she would never leave the farm again, and if the child ever dared to call him grandpa, he would kill it on the spot. The older sisters said that if she never left the place again, neither would they.

The daughter eventually gave birth to a boy, and the family kept him hidden from the community until he was about ten years old. Then one day he was helping his grandfather dig a hole, and getting excited, he called the old man "grandpa", whereupon, the old man killed him with his shovel and buried him there. The small grave was visible for many years, I was told, but today is under the concrete of a highway that cuts through the area. True to their word, none of the sisters ever married or left the old home place.

I grew up hearing stories such as these. It was all part of the legend of the backwoods, and during the hard times of the Depression years, they absorbed our attention and gave us something to think about besides the most obvious, which was how to survive our harsh lives.

One thing that happened during the Depression gave the countryside something to talk about for a while. We lived near a railroad cut, which sliced through the mountain about a mile from our home. One Sunday afternoon, a carload of people from the next county whose driver had been sipping a bit of moonshine, missed the mountain curve above the cut, and went over the side. It was about a hundred feet down, and how any of them survived is a mystery. Actually, they all survived except the driver, who tried to jump out of the car, and was crushed under it. The car was an old Buick, and everyone said that i was the "body by Fisher", which Buick was famous for, that saved the rest of the group.

In most parts of the world, this incident might not have been considered remarkable, but in our community, where there was little to talk about, it was a catastrophe of great magnitude. It provided many hours of wonder at the seemingly miraculous survival of all but one of these people.

Our diversions were few, so ghost stories, crimes and accidents gave us something to talk about.

XIV

Mama, I Sewed My Finger!

When I was very small, I began sewing doll clothes with a needle and thread. I was never allowed to use the sewing machine for fear I might run the needle through my finger. The sewing machine was an ancient treadle type that my parents had bought second hand in the early days of their marriage, and it was the only sewing machine we ever had. My mother made all of our clothes until my sister and I were old enough to sew. She made everything we all wore except my father's pants and shirts, and the boys' denim overalls. She always whistled when she was sewing. At first she never used a pattern, since that was the way she had learned, growing up. I began making my own clothes when I was thirteen, which was right in the middle of the Depression. My sister had already been doing her own for several years. Dress material was very cheap: we could get enough good material for a dress for about thirty-five cents. Patterns were a dime, and we would use the same pattern several times, changing it a bit with each use. Our underclothes and sleeping outfits were made from feed sacks.

The old sewing machine was also put to good use piecing quilt tops. My mother had long since ceased to have time to piece quilt tops by hand, so the job was done by machine. When the quilt top was finished, she would manage to get a cotton bat for the padding, make a lining from feed sacks, put up her quilting frames, whang the quilt to them, and be ready to quilt. Quilting a quilt by hand would usually take about two weeks. She did beautiful quilting.

We also used a lot of dye in those days. The beautiful printed feed sacks that we got, were not suitable for some things, so we would dye the plain ones for such jobs. I remember once my mother sewed a whole wardrobe of shirts for my father from feed sacks that she had dyed. He received quite a few compliments on them.

About the only things we didn't make on the sewing machine were our shoes and stockings. Our stockings we bought on the cheap and made them last. Our shoes we mended with kits bought at the five and dime store. Each kit contained two rubber shoe soles and a tube of cement with which to affix the soles to the shoes. The soles came in several sizes and we used a lot of them. The men also bought metal taps to put on the heels and toes of their shoes to keep them from wearing out. They made quite a noise as they went click clicking across the floor. The sound of the clunky leather heels that many shoes have today reminds me of those days.

I always liked to dance, although it was strictly forbidden by the conservative religions of the era. Even as a child, I was always moving, trying to perfect a few clogging steps I had learned at school. Our father was constantly upbraiding me for always moving around and wearing out my shoes.

In those days, we always used oilcloth tablecloths except when the preacher came to dinner, then we used damask. My mother always kept one nice white damask cloth for that purpose. For family meals, oilcloth worked best because the kids were constantly spilling things, and we had a great deal of laundry to do, without a week's worth of tablecloths. Some of the oilcloths were very pretty, with their bright colors and appropriate designs. We never used napkins because of the extra laundry involved. Our flatware was eclectic, to put it kindly. Some of what we had was cheap silver-plate, which quickly deteriorated. Some of the rest had composition handles, which soon came off if left in the dishwater a bit too long. Our knives, because of the kids and the destructive ways they found in which to use them, were usually "big butch, little butch, no handle, and shackleback", as the country saying goes. In other words, we hardly had any good knives most of the time. Our dishes were mostly Depression glass. It was given as bonuses with the purchase of gasoline, and my father over the years brought home a ton of it. He always chose the "lace" design in pink, so at least our dishes always matched. It was good he kept getting them, since being glass; many of them were quickly broken at our house. Today, they would have some value, if we still had them.

I remember one time my father came home very upset because a service station manager where he always bought, and with whom he had thought he had a very good relationship, had really chewed him out. Gasoline was only a few cents a gallon then, but a large truck takes many gallons. My father (probably having just sold a load of cows) paid the man with a twenty-dollar bill, at which the man went into a tirade. Probably the least offensive of what he said was, "What do you think I am a bank?" He probably had opened the station that morning with a few small bills, and was depending on the one-dollar and two-dollar purchases trickling in to build it up, and my father wrecked his plan. I suppose that paying with a twenty-dollar bill at that time would be the equivalent of paying with a thousand-dollar bill today. For a person brought up in and conditioned to this kind of economic environment, it has been a long journey into today's world and the present economic environment. The Depression kids have had to run hard to keep up with the changes, which were begun by their own generation at the end of World War II.

XV

Goober Salve Sandwiches and Seven Year Itch

There were no free breakfasts or lunches at school then, as there are in some places today. Therefore, those who couldn't afford the nickel a made-from-government-surplus lunch would cost in the lunchroom brought whatever they had at home. I only ate in the lunchroom once during my high school career. I usually did without lunch, since, as I've already said, our father didn't like to buy sliced bread, and I was ashamed to take biscuits in my lunch in high school. In grade school, I hadn't minded.

One day, I had gotten a nickel somewhere, and when the homeroom teacher asked who was going to the lunchroom, I held up my hand. Witch that she was, she couldn't let it pass, but said, "oh we're getting prosperous, aren't we?!" Oh, how I despised that woman! Once I got there, however, I realized that eating in the lunchroom was no big deal. The lunch consisted of butterbeans, cornbread, and just a dab of cole slaw. I never cared to eat there again, afford it or not.

During the Depression I saw people put some strange things between two slices of bread and call it a sandwich. When I was in grade school, many students brought fried squirrel or fried rabbit, fried side meat of pork, or potted meat sandwiches. Potted meat is canned meat on the order of pate. A butcher friend of mine told me that it is not the healthiest thing to eat, being made from the least desirable parts of beef, pork and chicken. During the Depression, school children ate prodigious amounts of it between slices of cheap white bread. Quite often the people who had chickens would boil two or three eggs and mix them with a can of potted meat to improve the taste and make it go further. Other times they would use the eggs to make egg salad sandwiches. Peanut butter sandwiches were standard, also. Peanut butter was called "goober salve", being made from "goobers", which is another name for peanuts, and having more or less the consistency of a salve. It is a very good protein, and people ate tons of it during the Depression, just as they do today.

Where school lunches were concerned, the operative words seemed to be "sliced bread". If one had sliced bread, white, cheap and non-nutritious though it might be, almost any food, beans, potato chips, mayonnaise, sorghum syrup, or just butter and sugar, could be put between the slices to make an acceptable sandwich. When I heard my mother talk about the lunches she carried to school, I realized that school lunches have always posed a problem. The standard school lunch in her day consisted of a gallon syrup bucket or lard bucket with about an inch of sorghum syrup on the bottom, and a wedge of cornbread and perhaps a baked sweet potato dropped into the syrup. My mother grew up healthy and lived to an advanced old age, but in my opinion it couldn't have been because of the school lunches she ate.

When I was in school during the Depression, everyone wrapped their lunches in newspapers. This posed another problem for me. The newspaper was not delivered where we lived, and the only way to get one was through the U.S. mail, in which case the news would be at least a day old. Consequently, we never had any newspapers, and I never had a lunchbox, as many of the students did. Therefore, just wrapping a lunch (on the occasions when I did take one) posed a problem. My father finally began buying paper bags for that purpose, but that wasn't until much later.

In the period of which I am writing, most working men took their lunches from home, just as many still do today. The going wage for a working man was a dollar a day. There were no fast food places where a workman could stop and get breakfast, and no lunch stands in the factories and mills, and no lunch trucks that came at noon each day. However, a small glass of peanut butter could be had for a nickel, and a small box of crackers for another nickel, and many a workman, and many a traveler got through the day on ten cents worth of "goober salve", and crackers. The small peanut butter glasses could be found everywhere along the roadsides.

Cookies of different kinds, such as gingersnaps and vanilla wafers, were also sold in nickel boxes. These were a favorite of the school kids, who would buy them at the small store that for many years stood on the edge of our school grounds. The proprietor also sold a variety of penny candies, and a few school supplies, such as pencils and writing tablets. I remember the taffy candies called "kisses" that sold two for a penny and were a favorite of the students. Another kind, a round candy, always had a marble inside. At that time the boys' favorite schoolyard game was marbles, and each boy tried to collect as many pretty marbles as he could, but always had one special, especially pretty one which he called his "toy", or "aggie". The marbles that were concealed in the candies were just cheap clay, gaily painted things, used only by the players who could not afford better quality. They were mostly just a good way for an unsuspecting child to break a tooth.

I have heard of students bringing clay to school to chew on during the day, but I confess I have never seen this. Such a thing I am sure would have been reported to the county health department. We had a county nurse who came to our school on a regular basis. She would register our height and weight, look at our teeth, and inspect our scalps to see if we had lice. Poor as everyone was at the time, I never knew anyone who had head lice. Scabies, however, did break out in our school, and I was amazed to see who had it and apparently were too poor to buy a tin of ointment to cure it, as they continued scratching year after year. No one in our family ever caught it.

I was always underweight, as were many in my class during the Depression years. I doubt that it was from not enough food, at least in my case. I'm sure it was because our family all had to work so incredibly hard, there was no chance of any fat accumulating on our frames. The long walk to school and back home each day also burned whatever calories might have been excessive or conducive to fat.

Sometimes the county nurse would give us shots. I remember once, just as the Depression was beginning the teacher told us one day that the nurse would be there the next day to vaccinate for smallpox, and to bring a note from home if our parents wanted us to be vaccinated. My mother wrote a note, of course, and at school I was very surprised to see that I was one of only two students who had brought notes. The other student was also a girl. We got our vaccinations, and mine festered slightly, but then healed, made a small scar, and I was presumably forever protected from smallpox. The other girl however, developed a terribly angry looking sore the size of a silver dollar, and it didn't heal for weeks.

The usual assortment of contagious diseases made the rounds at our school during the Depression years. Everyone, by the time they were in the third grade would usually have had measles, chicken pox, and mumps. I suppose I had the measles, although I don't remember it. I never had the mumps. My experience with chicken pox consisted merely of a few itchy red pimples here and there on my body. I told my mother, and she said "it's just the meanness working out of you", and that was that. A few days later, my older sister broke out in a full-blown case of the disease, and oh, the complaining and blaming it on me for bringing it home. I suppose it never occurred to anyone that she might have caught it the same place I did.

No rare or deadly disease ever broke out at our small county schools, as sometimes happens in the large city schools today. We never had any tuberculosis that anyone knew of, we never had any meningitis, and we never had anything except the ordinary childhood diseases mentioned above. Perhaps that can be attributable to the way we lived. Our bodies being daily exposed to a myriad of pathogens, I think perhaps our immune systems' strength rose proportionately and protected us. We had no sanitation. The water we drank came from springs or shallow wells and was probably contaminated. Innumerable chickens, ducks, turkeys, guineas, sometimes goats, and always several dogs shared the yard where we played. We had no hot water except what we could heat in an iron kettle that alternately sat on the cookstove, or in the fireplace, wherever there was a fire at any given moment. In the wintertime, the house was inadequately heated by one fireplace and my sister and I slept in a room that was never heated at any time. We drank whole, unpasteurized milk, just as it came from the cow, ate gobs of butter, fatty pork and the vital organs of beef.

Because of the grain and other feeds we kept for the farm animals, we always were overrun with huge rats. Except on rare occasions, we managed to keep them out of the house, but their droppings were everywhere. Mice would get into our house and build their nest in our clothes, quilts, linens, or anywhere they could remain hidden long enough to build a nest and have a litter of little ones.

When it rained, the runoff from the cattle barn the chicken house and the pigpen came down on us, and probably found it's way into our drinking water. During the warm months, usually from March until October, we had to deal with the flies. We had screens on the windows and doors, but with a household of ten or eleven people, the doors were constantly being opened and shut, and flies would get in. It was a problem, not only at mealtime, but if one wanted to take a nap, or just sit and read. Considering all the germs flies are known to carry, it's a wonder we weren't all sick more than we were.

Combine all of this with the lack of medical care, the hard work we had to do on a daily basis. Then, think of the long walks to school in the cold and rain, and one can get an idea of how our bodies had to fight to keep us well.

We never worried about everything in our environment not being germ free. An old saying went "you have to eat a peck of dirt before you die", and since a peck of dirt is a good bit of dirt, we didn't worry about dying young, either. However, not every family was as fortunate as ours. In addition to scabies, as was mentioned earlier, it was not uncommon to see a student with a case of ringworm on his or her face or arms. One adult that I knew of in our community and probably many more that I didn't know of, had pellagra for many years, caused from protein-deficient diets. The health of many people, especially children and young people, was forever damaged by the privations of the Great Depression.

XVI

Ridge Runners and Bootlegger Turnarounds

Bootlegging has been mentioned several times in previous chapters. This mode of endeavor was so widespread in the area in which I grew up, one could hardly write about the era without dwelling on it. Many otherwise honest and law abiding people under the circumstances of the time, turned to this illegal pursuit. Morals and ethics were of lesser importance when hunger entered the situation. At the risk of being considered an apologist for an illegal activity, I must say that in some cases I understand their plight. If a man had a large family, as almost everyone did at that time, and only a few worn-out acres on which to make a living when their steel mill jobs played out, I can understand his doing whatever he had to do to keep his family fed. Usually there was nothing left but to turn to "making", as it was called. Considering the unpopularity of the Volstead Act, many people didn't consider that they were doing anything patently illegal.

In the area where we lived, it was a given that a good percentage of the people lived by making and selling illegal booze. Even with this knowledge, we still had some surprises. I remember once a family moved into a rental house very close to us. They seemed to be good, working class people determined to make a living on the acreage they had rented along with the house. Since they had children the same age as us, we became good friends. Then one day we were walking in the nearby woods when we came upon a whiskey still. It was so near their house, we knew it had to be theirs. We filed that intelligence away and never told anyone, and the family soon moved away. They evidently had moved there with good intentions, but found that they couldn't make a living on the place, and facing daily hunger gave up and moved away. We hadn't known they were that desperate. The oldest son came back to visit us once, many years later.

Many others of our neighbors made and sold whiskey all during the Depression, and were never molested. We heard that it was because they regularly made payments to the local authorities. Others were caught and sent away to the state penitentiary for a year and a day. Neighbors were always "turning up" their neighbors to the law, thus adding to the bad feeling in the community. It was a grossly unfair and unsatisfactory system.

As mentioned in a previous chapter, our father always bought sugar for our large family; in one hundred-pound bags as a way of saving money and extra trips to town. The bootleggers also purchased sugar in one hundred pound bags. I don't know if someone had reported my father because of this, or if it was pure malice, although we always suspected the latter. In any event, the local law enforcement came to our house one day and searched the place for whiskey. They didn't search for a still, as was the usual procedure, but searched our house from top to bottom. As already said, it was a flawed and unfair system. Our father always did well with his farming and cattle, and he always minded his own business, and didn't interfere with the bootleggers, so it had to be a case of jealousy or pure malice.

On a summer evening at twilight, we could stand on the hill above our house and see smoke rising in the hollows roundabout where the "shiners" were "cooking off" their mashpots. They usually did their cooking at night, to avoid detection. After filling the mashpot with sugar, meal, and water, they would allow it to sit for a number of days until fermentation had taken place. Then a fire under the mashpot would start it cooking, and the lid on the pot would direct the fumes into a copper tube called the "worm". Through this tube, the fumes were directed into a container where they were condensed into alcohol. From here, the moonshine alcohol was put into containers of every description, everything from Coca-Cola bottles to Mason fruit jars, to jugs of all sizes up to five gallons. Then it was ready to be sold.

This was before the advent of panel trucks or pickups with toppers. In this situation and in the interest of speed and maneuverability, the chosen mode of the bootleggers was touring cars with large trunks. To have a large trunk, one had to have a large, expensive car. Considering the economy of the times, however, the once expensive cars were virtually "junkers", by the time they became affordable to the bootleggers. Then, they were likely to be "souped up" to the extent of the knowledge and ability of some local shade-tree mechanic to insure maximum speed, for outrunning the revenue officers required it.

The "runners" who delivered the whiskey to the customers, or the middleman, as the case might be, had the most dangerous job of all. They had to be skilled drivers, and to know how to do a 'bootlegger's turnaround" successfully. To execute this escape maneuver, the driver, while going at a considerable speed, would slam on the brakes, shift into reverse while rapidly turning the wheel to the right, then the left, then gunning the motor. Then he was off down the road meeting the revenue officers going in the opposite direction, it had all been done so quickly. It was the bootleggers' favored mode of escape, and the lonely mountain roads that the ridgerunners traveled were ideal for such shenanigans.

If a runner happened to be caught with his illegal load, the whiskey was confiscated, and presumably poured out on the ground. The driver was sent to the 'Big House" (the state penitentiary) for the standard year and a day. There, he most likely would be put to work on a rockpile, making little rocks out of big ones, as the expression went. The chirt road in front of our house was always worked by state prisoners. They had to pound the large chunks of chirt with sledgehammers until they were of a size that automobiles could travel over them.

A bootlegger always had a watchman, whose duty it was to keep watch around the still when any work was going on. He usually would sit on a knoll away from the still, which was always in a hollow, for security and access to water. From his perch, he could watch the surrounding woods and listen for the approach of any intruder or especially, any revenue officers. If you happened to inadvertently approach one of these watchmen in the woods, it was wise to greet them, tell them you were lost, (whether you were or not), and proceed in another direction.

Generally, we sympathized with the bootleggers. Almost without exception, they were merely trying to make a living in the only way that was left open to them in the economic climate of the Great Depression. They were desperately trying to feed their families. As a family, therefore, we minded our own business, hoed our peas and gathered our corn, and didn't concern ourselves with what our neighbors were doing. What we did object to was the social mayhem that drinking of the wildcat whiskey caused. There were numerous shootings in the community as a result of bootleggers drinking their own product.

XVIII

Added Memories

As I was talking with my sister recently, our conversation, as it nearly always does, eventually came around to the years of hard work and deprivation known as the Great Depression. No one who lived through that terrible decade could have failed to be traumatized by it. The experience shaped an entire generation. However, it made us tough, both mentally and physically, which can be useful as one goes through life.

She mentioned how our mother fed so many hungry travelers who came to our door, from the road, the railroad, and sometimes from the community. She never turned anyone away, and always did her good deeds with a smile and a few words of encouragement. Many of these people had traveled very great distances on foot. I remember once, one of my father's first cousins and his wife walked from Alabama to Texas, hoping to find a better economic situation out there. It didn't happen, of course, so they eventually walked back. I can only hope that some kind soul fed them along the way.

Also mentioned was how our schoolmates would put cardboard in their shoes when holes wore in the soles. Then when the cardboard wore out, they would replace it with more on and on, until the soles were completely gone, and there was nothing to hold the cardboard. We never had to do this. Our father always made sure we had shoes for the long walk to school over the chirt road. Many of the students whose parents worked in the mines and mills, and were only getting to work one or two days per week, were not so lucky. Any such experience is sure to either break a young person's spirit, or make them incredibly strong. I think in all the cases that we knew of, it did the latter. The generation of young people that came out of the Great Depression, though battered and scarred, were tough as mule meat, as the saying goes.

I had forgotten that there were instances where people went into our corncrib and shucked out a pillowcase full of corn to take to the grist mill to be ground into meal. I mentioned in a previous chapter that they sometimes went into our cornfield and gathered and shucked corn to take to the grist mill and left the shucks lying between the cornrows. I hadn't remembered that they actually went into our corncrib, which was very near the house. It must have been someone who was a frequent visitor at our house. Otherwise, our dogs would have eaten them alive, or at least aroused the household. However, when people are hungry, personal safety takes a lower priority. I suppose I'm glad that we never at the time knew about the theft, or the identity of the perpetrator. We could well afford to lose a bushel of corn. We didn't have any disposable cash, but we did have corn.

Another thing that was mentioned in our conversation was how our mother began cutting our father's hair, as well as the boys. Haircuts didn't cost much at that time, of course, but it was that much that we could avoid spending. Our father brought home a pair of hand clippers, and she began cutting their hair and keeping all of them neat and well groomed. She did a very good job of it until my father's death, and the youngest brother left home. I must admit, I do the same thing today, although I have electric clippers rather than the hand operated kind. I have cut my husband's hair for most of our married life. He prefers it that way. I suppose that once a Depression kid, always a Depression kid.

My sister mentioned all the different animals we had during the Depression. Besides the usual dogs and cats, the milk cows, the horse, pigs, and chickens, we had goats, turkeys, guineas, ducks, and geese. I seem to remember that at one time we even had a pair of pea fowls just because they were pretty. This all meant work, of course, but I always enjoyed being around the animals. People from town would often throw unwanted pets out of their cars near our house, knowing that we would probably take them in. Since our father butchered, there were always bones to chew, and our mother always cooked extra for the dogs. Some of the best dogs we ever had were abandoned pets that came to us out of the woods. Sometimes, however, the pets that were thrown out of cars continued to live in the woods and eventually became feral, and were very dangerous. Once a pack of them attacked one of our yard dogs and killed it.

As already mentioned, we nearly always raised peanuts during the Great Depression. I had forgotten that we made our own peanut butter, but my sister mentioned it. We didn't have a Cuisinart, or any of the fancy kitchen gadgets that are so common today (no electricity, remember). We would parch the peanuts in a biscuit pan in the oven, shell them, and run them through the same hand-operated grinder that we used to grind the pork sausage at hog-killing time. I don't remember much about this homemade peanut butter, but it probably was as good as what could be bought in the stores at that time. The store-bought kind was not homogenized, and the oil would rise to the top, making it necessary to re-mix it before each use, or deal with a sticky inedible blob once the topmost inch or so was gone.

Our parents were, above all, generous. They showed this in many ways, not only during the Depression, but throughout their lives, my sister, however, mentioned one thing in particular that she remembered from the Depression. She remembered how our parents would always divide the fresh pork with our neighbors at hog butchering time in the fall. We always killed several hogs at one time, so we could do this without any great hardship. Our neighbors, on the other hand, always repaid us in good will and help when we needed it. As already mentioned, our neighbor lady was with my mother at the birth of several of her children, although my sister said that she had that duty at the birth of the youngest one. My sister was nineteen at the time.

As we talked, we each wondered how our family survived, and how we came out of this experience with our spirits intact, still believing in a better tomorrow, and still anxious to take advantage of opportunities when they finally came.

XVIII

What It All Meant

The greatest motivator in the world is hunger. The businessman is hungry for money. The great actress is hungry for adulation. The baseball player is hungry for a winning season. So it goes with all of us. Anyone, who achieves any great success in life, begins with a devouring hunger to succeed. The generation that emerged from the Great Depression was hungry. After enduring years of physical hunger and grinding deprivation, they were hungry for a chance in life. After having to give up their dreams of college as teenagers, they were hungry to make up for lost time and still get an education, as many of them did. Then they were hungry to see their children get the best education possible. They were hungry to see their towns and cities, long wallowing in stagnation become vibrant centers of culture. In short, they were poised to do great things, if only given the chance.

Then came the big war. A whole generation of young men was called up, from the farms, the city streets, and from the reservations. Many Navajos, who later gained fame as the Code Talkers, came wearing pigtails to the chairs of military barbers. Poor boys from every background, who often had never been more than a few miles from their own front doors, were sent to the far corners of the world. **For many, in spite of the dangers, it opened up a new world where there was enough food and sufficient clothing, and where one could see a doctor when necessary**. Many of these young men due to the privations of the Depression era in which they had grown up, had never been to a dentist until they were called into the military. Many of these kids who had never had any kind of a chance in life, died in the moment of their greatest prosperity. The ones who survived the carnage came home with a vision of a better life than the one they had left.

Through the GI Bill, many thousands were given a chance at a college education, something they could never have hoped for before. Many, who otherwise would never have gotten away from the farms or the mills, became dentists, teachers, and other professionals. They married, built homes, and raised families. They worked and paid taxes, and the combined effect was to propel the United States into an era of prosperity they had not known before. Eventually they built our country into the greatest, most powerful nation the world has ever known.

Along the way some were called to serve their country a second time, this time in the political arena. We have seen them serve in all areas, from the lowest position in local politics, to the highest office in the land. We have also seen a flowering of literary and musical genius, and prowess in the Olympic world. It might not have happened had someone not built a firm platform from which the succeeding generations could spring, and this platform was education.

 All they needed was a chance, this horde of hungry, kids from the Depression era, and once given a chance, they made the most of it. We hear our government criticized on occasion and sometimes perhaps deservedly, but in the case of the GI Bill, someone was gifted with unusual foresight, and deserves a great deal of credit. Also, once started, this tradition has continued, and our military continues to help their enlistees further their education. If, as we are told, education is the key to great things, the great nation that the Depression kids built will continue to prosper far into the future.

My father and his cattle truck. This was the sole transportation for the family. We were no strangers to bovine scatology.

My father's slaughtering house in ruins. My sister and I spent many a cold morning here helping skin out and saw down beef.

My brother-in-law, Walter Carter, plowing the garden for planting.

These are two of my mother's "depression babies." Evie, on the right, born in 1931, and Jim, born in 1933.

This is how our house appeared during the depression.

The same house, remodeled after the depression.

My mother (on the right) and sister Velma resting during one of our fishing trips to Lily Shoals on Cahaba River.

Cahaba River, as it appeared back then.

The author, wading in Cahaba River during a fishing trip.

My parents, honest, hard-working country people.

The Seales siblings in 1929, when the depression started. Left to right we are Velma, Madge, Joe, and Gene. I didn't look very happy. I grew up angry and resentful because of the way we had to live, the lack of educational and cultural opportunities, and the general unfairness of life.

This is my father (on the left) visiting a sick friend in the VA Hospital in Tuscaloosa. My father had a rough exterior, but a soft heart, and was very compassionate.

This was my uncle, Monroe Porter, my mother's brother. He would arise early and kill squirrels for our breakfast.

My brothers Joe and Gene, new military recruits. Until their enlistment, neither had been more than thirty miles from home.

My mother, standing outside the house we grew up in.

My brothers Joe (left) at age five, and Gene (right), age three, ready for church.

My brothers Joe (top), age 10, Gene (right), age 8, and Bill, age 6, in 1935.

My sister Velma in 1934, the year she graduated from high school. Everyone was so poor, the class couldn't afford pictures for an annual, so someone made profiles of the graduates and they cobbled them together a homemade book of remembrances.

My brother Bill with his school bus. The job paid fifteen dollars a month, a fortune for anyone in my family's circumstances.

My mother at "Eight Acre Rocks," in Tuscaloosa County, where she was born.

My grandfather, my mother's father.

Two of my father's aquaintances.

My brother Gene at about age three. Even their childish games
somehow always involved cows.

My precious mother and my
precious daughter.

Our family, after surviving the depression. My husband and I were
leaving for three years in Paris the next day, and my mother had cooked
dinner for the entire family. After dinner I shooed everyone into one
corner and snapped this picture. Our family is more than twice this size
now and most have done extremely well. We were a strong family
already, and the depression only made us stronger.